Understanding the End Times

Sounding the trumpet of readiness to the end-time church

Archbishop Nicholas Duncan-Williams

A GOSHEN PUBLISHERS BOOK   VIRGINIA

Understanding the End Times
Sounding the trumpet of readiness to the end-time church

ISBN-13: 978-0-9994003-5-7
Copyright ©2019 Nicolas Duncan-Williams

All rights reserved solely by the author. The author guarantees all contents are original and do not infringe upon the legal rights of any other person or work. No part of this book may be reproduced, shared in a retrieval system, or transmitted in any form or by any means, electronic, mechanical, photocopying, and recording, without prior written permission of the Publisher.

Published in 2019 by:

GOSHEN PUBLISHERS LLC
P.O. Box 1562
Stephens City, Virginia, USA
www.GoshenPublishers.com

Cover Design by GOSHEN PUBLISHERS LLC

For further inquiries and for training materials, please email Agents@GoshenPublishers.com.

10 9 8 7 6 5 4 3 2 1

Contents

Introduction 1

1. Jesus' 2nd Coming: Myth or Reality? 5
    Jesus' Declaration 6
    The Testimony of the Angels 9
    Peter's Testimony 10

2. Signs of the End times: Jesus' Teaching 15
    The Destruction of the Temple 19
    Relocation of the Capital to Jerusalem 19
    Rebuilding of the Temple 20
    Hardships and Strange Happenings 21
    False Prophets and False Christs 22
    Believe not Every Spirit 24
    Kingdoms against Kingdoms 27
    Betrayals 29
    The Days of Noah are with us 30

3. Signs of the End Times: the Apostles' Teaching 35
    Lovers of Themselves 37
    Covetous 38
    Boasters 39
    Disobedient to Parents 41
    Unthankful 42
    Without Natural Affection 44
    Lovers of Pleasure More than Lovers of God 46
    Departures from the Faith 48

4. What Occupies You Today? 51
    Where is your Mind? 51
    Where is your Treasure? 54
    Beware of a Glittering World 56
    Where's your Christian Commitment? 58

5. Where is Your Soul-winning Fire? 61
    Jesus on Winning the Lost 62
    What has Happened to that Fire? 64

6. Ready for Flight H-E-A-V-E-N? 71
  - Spiritual Magnetism 73
  - Work Out your Own Salvation 76
  - Sanctification 78
  - Beware of Sexual Immorality 84

7. Don't be left Behind 89
  - Like a Thief in the Night 94
  - Be Wise and Redeem the Time 95
  - Pursue Peace and Holiness 98
  - Walk in Purity of Heart 101
  - Hold on to the End 103

8. What if You Miss the Rapture? 107
  - The Great Tribulation 107
  - Seven Plagues 109

9. Judgment after Death 119
  - Judgment Throne of God 121
  - Judgment Seat of Christ 124

Epilogue: My Foretaste of Heaven 129

Introduction

I carry a heavy burden in my heart that I would like to share with you. It is about the times we are living in. The whole world is experiencing what I would describe as a paradox.

Look around and you can see many things that were not thought of years back. Fifty years ago in my country, for example, no one talked about the gender of a child before it was born. Today, through technology, this can be known long before a baby is born.

Right from what happens in our kitchen to what happens in our business establishments and in our churches, progress in infrastructure stares us in the face. Some would opine that we have progressed from the ancient into the modern world.

The question to ask is this: How have all these translated into a life of peace, harmony, love, and brotherliness, and meaning for existence? And that is precisely where my heartache starts.

With all the developments around us, humanity is still struggling to live in harmony with the universe the way that

God intended. There is little peace even in those countries considered as very developed. Sometimes the social problems in those countries way exceed those in the countries that are considered as underdeveloped. In terms of a real and refreshing life of peace, and health and wellness of the human soul, the earth is still groping in darkness, with one dashed hope after the other.

We live in times and in days where radio and television stations report nothing good, but mostly evil reports. Natural disasters, such as earthquakes and hurricanes, occur almost every week, destroying entire communities and cities, and human lives and property, wiping them out in hundreds and thousands.

And, you wonder what is going on? Strange weather patterns, strange happenings, and strange incidents occur every minute. The imaginations and philosophies of men and women cannot make sense of events that are happening.

These occurrences are not going to get any better anywhere. Let the people who are living in developing countries of the world stop running for visas in the hope of migrating to other countries for improvement, because it is not going to get better anywhere. As a matter of fact, it is going to get worse.

The more I thought about these things the less sense it made, considering the noise being made about the achievements of humanity, sometimes to the exclusion of God.

Then the Lord began to minister to me about the end times. He drew my attention to the fact that He had spoken these things several years ago and the early church fathers also spoke about their happening. All these are tied to the Second Coming of Jesus Christ and the end of the world.

He got my attention and the reality began to hit me as never before. Out of that a sense of urgency captivated my spirit, concerning the coming of our Lord Jesus Christ. His coming is truly closer than we think. Then one thing led to another and I became concerned about the state of the church, particularly the fact that we are asleep while all these prophecies about the end times roll out before our eyes.

I am not a prophet of doom, but I have a moral and a spiritual responsibility to warn you so you can be armed. You cannot be ignorant. Ignorance is a luxury you and I cannot afford to indulge in, especially in times like these.

This is the burden that led me to publish this book. This is not a comprehensive teaching on eschatology like you would have it in a theological school. It is about a sense of urgency. It is a wakeup call. We have to wake up from slumber and do something before we all become irrelevant in God's agenda for the earth and eternity.

As you read this book, do so with urgency as if your whole life depends on it. Actually, your life depends on the responses you give to the issues I am addressing.

It is time again to sound the trumpet "Maranatha" and alert everyone under the sound of our voices that Jesus is truly coming again and very, very soon!

1.
JESUS' 2ND COMING: MYTH OR REALITY?

The end time (aka, "end times", "end of time", "last days", or "eschaton") is a future time-period described in eschatology. It teaches that world events will reach a final climax.

The question I want to address in this opening chapter is simple: *Is Jesus' Second Coming a myth or reality?* The answer to this question lies in the authenticity of the statement. Is Jesus' Second Coming someone's opinion, or is it a statement of substance?

> [1] *Let not your heart be troubled: ye believe in God, believe also in me.*
>
> [2] *In my Father's house are many mansions: if it were not so, I would have told you. I go to prepare a place for you.*
>
> [3] *And if I go and prepare a place for you, I will come again, and receive you unto myself; that where I am, there ye may be also.*
>
> (John 14:1-3)

JESUS' DECLARATION

Jesus' return is not a proposal; it is not an opinion expressed by the writers of the New Testament. It was a theme Jesus Himself introduced and taught. Do not let anyone deceive you that there is no Second Coming.

During the period preceding His betrayal, Jesus openly talked first about His exit of the world by death on a cross. This we know to be true because Peter rebuked Him for even thinking of dying. In return, Jesus rebuked him sharply.

In fact, the rebuke was to the devil. I am sure Peter did not understand why Jesus would say "Get thee behind me, Satan" (Matt 16:23), when it was Peter who was speaking.

Jesus did not only speak about His death on the cross, but He also spoke about His resurrection. He said that He had the power to lay down His life and take it again. Remember, it was one of the accusations made against Him at His trial.

Then Jesus talked about going back to heaven. He made it clear that He was going back home. Jesus spoke more about heaven than anyone else in the Bible.

In the process of talking about going to heaven, He taught His disciples about His coming back to the earth in very clear terms.

When Jesus started telling His disciples that He was about to leave, they became troubled. That is understandable. For three and a half years they had hidden behind Him against the pressures of their society.

No one could touch them because they were with the Man who had turned every man's world upside down by His teaching and the working of miracles. The Scribes and Pharisees could not handle Him because His deeds were known all over the world.

His disciples were not sure what was going to happen when Jesus left them, so Jesus had to break the ice with these comforting and powerful words: Jesus emphatically told His disciples that He would leave temporarily and that He would come back again.

Jesus sends a very important message to the church concerning testifying of Him. He could have just encouraged the believers to continue to testify of Him. Instead, He linked it up with the truth about His coming back to earth in the full glory of the Father and of His angels.

> *If anyone is ashamed of me and my words in this adulterous and sinful generation, the Son of Man will be ashamed of him when he comes in his Father's glory with the holy angels.*

(Mark 8:38)

Jesus always looked for opportunity to talk about His Second Coming. On one such occasion multitudes had gathered. Jesus taught on a variety of topics: warning them against the hypocrisy of the Pharisees; living in the light because everything will be exposed; never to worry about the things of this life; warning against speaking against the Holy Spirit; warning against covetousness; and then He dropped this bombshell about His coming:

> [36] *And ye yourselves like unto men that wait for their lord, when he will return from the wedding; that when he cometh and knocks, they may open unto him immediately.*
>
> [37] *Blessed are those servants, whom the lord when he cometh shall find watching: verily I say unto you, that he shall gird himself, and make them to sit down to meat, and will come forth and serve them.*
>
> [38] *And if he shall come in the second watch, or come in the third watch, and find them so, blessed are those servants.*
>
> [39] *And this know, that if the good man of the house had known what hour the thief would come, he would have watched, and not have suffered his house to be broken through.*

> ⁴⁰ Be ye therefore ready also: for the Son of man cometh at an hour when ye think not.
>
> (Luke 12:36-40)

On this occasion Jesus did not only teach emphatically about His coming again, but also urged His hearers to be ready at any time since no one knows when He will come back. I have expounded upon the readiness Jesus expects of us in another chapter of this book.

THE TESTIMONY OF THE ANGELS

Jesus' coming back again to the earth was affirmed at His ascension on the mount. This time it was by two angels who were present for that memorable event. The disciples looked up as Jesus ascended. The two angels addressed whatever was going on in their minds and hearts. This is the record of the angels' testimony

> ¹⁰ And while they looked steadfastly toward heaven as he went up, behold, two men stood by them in white apparel;
>
> ¹¹ Which also said, Ye men of Galilee, why stand ye gazing up into heaven? This same Jesus, which is taken up from you into heaven, shall

so come in like manner as ye have seen him go into heaven.

(Acts 1:10-11)

PETER'S TESTIMONY

The Apostle Peter exhorted the believers and warned also against scoffers whose goal is to derail the believers who are looking forward to Jesus' coming.

> 1 *This second epistle, beloved, I now write unto you; in both which I stir up your pure minds by way of remembrance:*
>
> 2 *That ye may be mindful of the words which were spoken before by the holy prophets, and of the commandment of us the apostles of the Lord and Savior:*
>
> 3 *Knowing this first, that there shall come in the last days scoffers, walking after their own lusts,*
>
> 4 *And saying, Where is the promise of his coming? for since the fathers fell asleep, all things continue as they were from the beginning of the creation.*

(2 Peter 3:1-4)

Peter, in his time, was conscious of scoffers and the goal of their activities. What he never ever wanted the believers to forget is the reality of the Second Coming of Jesus.

Way back then, he wrote as if he knew that today there would be people making a mockery of the fact of the return of our Lord Jesus Christ. Some have tried to brush it aside and live as if the whole thing is a myth.

Peter offered the reason Jesus had not come as of the time he was writing. It is to provide opportunity to many in the world to come back to Jesus. In other words, yield their lives to Jesus and become born again. This he explained as he continued his writing:

> 8 But, beloved, be not ignorant of this one thing, that one day is with the Lord as a thousand years, and a thousand years as one day.
>
> 9 The Lord is not slack concerning his promise, as some men count slackness; but is longsuffering to us-ward, not willing that any should perish, but that all should come to repentance.
>
> 10 But the day of the Lord will come as a thief in the night; in the which the heavens shall pass away with a great noise, and the elements shall melt with fervent heat, the earth also and the works that are therein shall be burned up.
>
> (2 Peter 3:8-10)

> **God's love for humanity is misunderstood to be His weakness. Whereas He was opening the door for many to come in before the door is shut, like in the time of Noah, men think otherwise and take the truth of Jesus' coming as a joke.**

We have the responsibility as believers to correct every error in human thinking concerning the coming of Jesus Christ.

The New Testament writers who wrote anything about the Second Coming all took their instructions from Jesus Himself.

> *But our citizenship is in heaven. And we eagerly await a Savior from there, the Lord Jesus Christ, who, by the power that enables him to bring everything under his control, will transform our lowly bodies so that they will be like his glorious body.*
>
> *(Philippians 3:20)*
>
> *Concerning the coming of our Lord Jesus Christ and our being gathered to him, we ask you, brothers, not to become easily unsettled or alarmed by some prophecy, report or letter supposed to have come from us, saying that the day of the Lord has already come.*

(2 Thessalonians 2:1-2)

Christ was sacrificed once to take away the sins of many people; and he will appear a second time, not to bear sin, but to bring salvation to those who are waiting for him.

(Hebrews 9:28)

Be patient, then, brothers, until the Lord's coming. See how the farmer waits for the land to yield its valuable crop and how patient he is for the autumn and spring rains. You too, be patient and stand firm, because the Lord's coming is near. Don't grumble against each other, brothers, or you will be judged. The Judge is standing at the door!

(James 5:7-9)

That is the critical message the world needs now. Jesus is coming again; sooner than we think. We have the responsibility as the representatives of God on earth to sound this alarm throughout the earth, pleading and urging people to give their lives to the Savior.

2.
SIGNS OF THE END TIMES: JESUS' TEACHING

The question that drives this chapter is this: "Are we in the last days?"

> *Of the sons of Issachar who had understanding of the times, to know what Israel ought to do, their chiefs were two hundred; and all their brethren were at their command;*
>
> *(1 Chronicles 12:32)*

We are living in very interesting times, and the enemy wants us to talk on prosperity, breakthrough, success, and every other thing except the coming of the Lord. He wants us to be ignorant of the times we live in and of the signs of the end time.

We can't afford to be ignorant because the maintenance of ignorance is the advantage of the adversary. We need to be enlightened. The Bible describes the sons of Issachar as men who had understanding of the times and knew what Israel should be doing at any time. We should be more sensitive and knowledgeable than they, because the Holy Spirit dwells in us.

The Bible gave several signs to signal to us the end of this current earth. It makes it clear that the current earth we live in, is on its way out; life on this earth is coming to an end. God's plan is to create a new heaven and a new earth (Rev 21:1).

God did not tell anyone the exact day when the earth will be folded up and packed away, and the new earth ushered in. Nevertheless, it gave several signs to signal to us the end of the earth.

In this chapter, I shall highlight a few of them. My goal is to revive the awareness of the reality of the end, a factor that is lost today because many of us are busy trying to save the earth and pursue our personal agendas.

When I heard about the possibility of moving the capital of Israel from Tel Aviv to Jerusalem, I said, "Okay, Lord, we have to start watching the clock." I never thought it would happen in my day, and that thought and imagination could not have even happened in the days of Barack Obama because he was too politically correct.

It had to take a man like Donald Trump, who has nothing to lose, to even think about that because the implications are heavy. No wonder president after president had shied away from it, until now.

I am not speaking from a political perspective because I am not a politician, and I am not speaking as the world speaks. Our language is different from theirs. Our rock is not their rock, our ways are not their ways, and our thoughts are not their thoughts. They think differently from us. We are in this world but not of the world.

It is believed by some school of thought that the major next event on planet earth will be the rapture. Apart from wars, rumors of wars, confusion and unrest and all the things that are happening, one major event that will happen next is the rapture.

One of the strategies of the enemy is to deceive and silence us, and when you start talking about these things, people think that you are preparing for your death, but I'm not dying yet. The truth is that some things need to be said to get the church ready.

In the 24th chapter of Matthew, Jesus taught comprehensively about the signs of the end times. Let the Scripture speak for itself:

> 3 And as he sat upon the mount of Olives, the disciples came unto him privately, saying, Tell us, when shall these things be? and what shall be the sign of thy coming, and of the end of the world?

⁴ And Jesus answered and said unto them, Take heed that no man deceive you.

⁵ For many shall come in my name, saying, I am Christ; and shall deceive many.

⁶ And ye shall hear of wars and rumours of wars: see that ye be not troubled: for all these things must come to pass, but the end is not yet.

⁷ For nation shall rise against nation, and kingdom against kingdom: and there shall be famines, and pestilences, and earthquakes, in divers places.

⁸ All these are the beginning of sorrows.

⁹ Then shall they deliver you up to be afflicted, and shall kill you: and ye shall be hated of all nations for my name's sake.

¹⁰ And then shall many be offended, and shall betray one another, and shall hate one another.

¹¹ And many false prophets shall rise, and shall deceive many.

¹² And because iniquity shall abound, the love of many shall wax cold.

¹³ But he that shall endure unto the end, the same shall be saved.

> ¹⁴ And this gospel of the kingdom shall be preached in all the world for a witness unto all nations; and then shall the end come.
>
> (Matthew 24:3-14)

Note that Jesus spoke on three things based on the questions that his disciples and apostles asked Him about the end of time. He spoke about the signs of the end of the world; not the end of the age, but the world. Jesus spoke about events and signs before, during, and after the rapture.

THE DESTRUCTION OF THE TEMPLE

One of the things Jesus said would happen is that the temple in Jerusalem would be brought down, and not a stone would remain on another. AD 70, General Titus moved into Jerusalem and brought down the temple.

RELOCATION OF THE CAPITAL TO JERUSALEM

The other is the capital moving from Tel Aviv to Jerusalem. If you follow events in the world news, you know that President Trump signed a document that declared Jerusalem to be the capital of Israel amidst a lot of opposition from world leaders; but it is happening and there will be no reversal. The nations that opposed will gradually come to acknowledge the move.

REBUILDING OF THE TEMPLE

The next sign would be the temple being built in Jerusalem. Interestingly, someone showed me something online recently. It is the temple of Solomon; it is about to be rebuilt and the plan and design is ready. The location is Jerusalem.

Now there are political, regional, national, and spiritual implications. The immediate is a possible conflict between the Jews and the Muslim world surrounding them because the site of the temple is currently the dome of the rock for the Muslim faith. The Jews are very hopeful of the rebuilding of the temple at that location, and some believe an earthquake may occur to demolish the dome of the rock.

Things will happen beyond the control and logic of man, and beyond the strength and the power of the region of the United Nations. It does not make sense. No one can manage these things because these are events that must happen that man has no control over.

> **We can debate it as much as we want but things will happen. God does not need the endorsement of any group of people on the face of the earth for these to happen. He is doing it according to His predetermined plan.**

I believe that if we live another 50 years, if Jesus tarries, the earth would destroy itself by man. Man is on a suicidal mission; we have pressed a button of self-destruction, and in the next 50 years, we ourselves would destroy the planet.

HARDSHIPS AND STRANGE HAPPENINGS

Jesus spoke of famines, pestilences, and earthquakes in diverse places.

This calls to mind some of the hurricanes and disasters, like what happened in Sierra Leone, where hundreds of people were buried in their homes. Strange happenings, strange incidences, strange weathers continually plague the earth. Some of these things are not just acts of Mother Nature. The Bible has explanation for them.

We hear of hurricanes and tsunamis. The sea was given an order by Elohim to not come into town; but these days the sea comes into town, wipes out a whole community and city, and goes back because it has to stay within its boundaries.

In Indonesia, for example, there have been all kinds of natural disasters, wiping out thousands of people. A recent plane crash about 13 minutes after the plane took off, killed hundreds of people, including children. It is becoming increasingly difficult to explain these happenings by mere human understanding.

FALSE PROPHETS AND FALSE CHRISTS

> [11] *And many false prophets shall rise, and shall deceive many.*
>
> [24] *For there shall arise false Christs, and false prophets, and shall shew great signs and wonders; insomuch that, if it were possible, they shall deceive the very elect.*
>
> *(Matthew 24:11, 24)*

Jesus said that many shall come in His name and say they are Christ and shall deceive many (Matt 24:5). Take note, He said not one or two false prophets, but many false prophets. Today we have a lot of them parading the corridors of

Christianity. There is one in my country who believes he can change into anything and change back into a human; and he still has people following him.

There are people who dare to call themselves Jesus, Son of God. That anyone should have the audacity to call himself Jesus is unthinkable. I am not talking about just using the name; these are saying that they are Jesus the Son of God, and they back their declaration by performing lying wonders and miracles.

Unfortunately, many people have developed itching ears and the false prophets are telling them what they want to hear. People are not enduring sound doctrine; they are giving heed to doctrines of devils.

They are still coming. They first of all get your attention by setting you up. They will tell you something that is going to happen to you, and then they will give you some direction that is not biblical. It is bait and what makes it dangerous is that what they tell the people is factual.

So, you have to be very careful when people say they have evidence, facts, and proof. They may have all these but it is all deceitful and aimed at getting you to go astray and hooked onto them instead of trusting God for yourself.

That is why Jesus said if it were possible these false prophets would deceive even the elect. So there is a possibility that the very elect can be deceived (Matt 24:24). If you study God's generals and look at different men and women God used so powerfully and mightily, and how the enemy deceived some, it just shows that you cannot put your confidence in a man. The reason history repeats itself is because people are not students of history.

Some years ago, there was a gentleman who used to be at one of the market squares in my city, named Peter. You should have seen the people who went to consult him; people in their own cars, and people of reputation and position.

This gentleman wouldn't even take a bath and was dressed like John the Baptist. People would go to see him and he would give them direction and some concoction to drink, and so on. In a matter of time, he suddenly disappeared.

Believe not Every Spirit

The Apostle John exhorted that we should not believe everyone who comes to us in the name of Jesus; and that we should actually test the spirits. Today, people are too desperate to verify if anyone is of God or not before they take in everything he or she says to them.

> *Beloved, do not believe every spirit, but test the spirits whether they are of God; because many false prophets have gone out into the world.*
>
> *(1 John 4:1)*

There are many spirits out there, but don't be fooled. There are so many gifted people, but many of them do not know sound doctrine. Some have a strong gift but they are not guided with knowledge. That makes them vulnerable to being misled, and some end up going into serious error, together with their followers.

You have to understand that what works in the realm of the spirit is like a key. You can take my car key and go to the car park and use my key on my car and my car will not call you a thief. The car will respond to the key. You can then move the car anywhere you want to, but you will be arrested eventually because it is not yours and I will report you to the authorities.

In the realm of the spirit you can operate by the name of Jesus and things will happen because at the mention of His name, every knee of things in heaven and on earth and under the earth shall bow, and every tongue shall confess that Jesus Christ is Lord.

So people who are described as "using the name of Jesus" are clearly not of Jesus. We don't use Jesus' name; He uses us as His instruments of His divine agenda.

Their churches increase in number by mischief, by manipulation, by exploitation and it is a matter of time; those churches dwindle and fade away. You can't scatter one church and gather yours and say you are working for the Lord. You are an enemy of the kingdom.

For it is written in Matthew 7:22, "Many will say to me in that day, Lord, Lord, have we not prophesied in thy name? and in thy name have cast out devils? and in thy name done many wonderful works?" And Jesus said, and I will say to you, you used the key to spark my car; you are a thief. Jesus called them workers of iniquity.

Jesus will say to them: "You worked against Me; you used My name to fight My work; you used My name to destroy what I was building through others. You were building a church not because I called you to win souls; you were doing it as an industry, to make money; to exploit people; to have a name; to become relevant.

You did those things not because I called, chose, or anointed you, you workers of iniquity. And I say to you, get thee hence from Me; I know you not".

KINGDOMS AGAINST KINGDOMS

Jesus said kingdoms will rise against kingdoms:

> For nation shall rise against nation, and kingdom against kingdom: and there shall be famines, and pestilences, and earthquakes, in divers places.
>
> (Matthew 24:7)

Look at the confusions in Yemen, Syria, and Saudi Arabia, and look at the situation with Iran and America, America and China, and America and Russia; these are situations of perpetual unrest.

Kingdom against kingdom also means political parties fighting against each other. That is the kind of society we have become. Kingdoms rising against kingdoms is just the beginning.

It is going to be brother against brother, sister against sister, husband against wife, wife against husband, children against parents, parents against children, and community against community. This kind of situation is going to escalate. These are just the beginning of sorrows.

I am not a prophet of doom, but I have a moral responsibility to equip and prepare you so events do not overtake you. It seems we are living a careless life, living ignorantly hoping for everything to get okay. It is not going to get better.

I am just telling you. If you look at the Scriptures carefully, Jesus predicted that these things would happen and the only assurance you and I have to face the future without fear, is His promises, including coming back for His own.

We cannot derive confidence from material wealth, "for a man's life consisteth not in the abundance of the things which he possesseth" (Luke 12:15).

If any man should boast of anything, please do not boast of your accomplishment or your education; your connections, your accesses, your family background, or whom you know; but this one thing – that you know the Lord, who executes judgment, righteousness, and justice upon the earth.

Betrayals

And then shall many be offended, and shall betray one another, and shall hate one another.

(Matthew 24:10)

You talk about offences; heavy offences are in the church. Right now there are people offended about what I am saying. They are asking themselves, "Why does he have to say all these things? Why doesn't he just talk about something that will encourage and lift us up, instead of all these frightening things?"

I am not frightening you; I am equipping you with knowledge and understanding for tomorrow. I want you to have understanding of the times. You cannot be in charge like the sons of Isaachar if you are ignorant of the times.

People are so easily offended, and if you do not understand that offences is one of the signs of the end time you will be so offended that if you are not careful you will backslide. I live with offences every day. I have gotten used to them. I have learned the skill of mastering offences.

When you talk about betrayals, it is heavy in the church. Christians betray Christians. Husbands betray their wives, and wives betray their husbands. Children betray their parents. It is all happening in the church.

We have become gamblers. In many countries, the citizens gamble every four years, taking all kinds of risks, putting out all kinds of monies into the system for political favors. Instead of doing the right thing, they want shortcuts to everything, and for some it means supporting and helping a political party come to power hoping that they will be rewarded when the party wins power.

Unfortunately, the betrayals and offences have infiltrated the church. There are people in the church who hate others in the same church. Meanwhile, you should hear them praying and speaking in tongues! You will hear earthquakes as if God has landed here on earth. One wonders what kinds of tongues those are.

People get shocked when they hear all these things and wonder why, as Christians, we do hateful things to each other. It is one of the things marking the beginning of sorrows.

THE DAYS OF NOAH ARE WITH US

Let us look at another rendition of Jesus concerning the signs of the end times

³⁷ But as the days of Noah were, so shall also the coming of the Son of man be.

³⁸ For as in the days that were before the flood they were eating and drinking, marrying and giving in marriage, until the day that Noah entered into the ark,

³⁹ And knew not until the flood came, and took them all away; so shall also the coming of the Son of man be.

⁴⁰ Then shall two be in the field; the one shall be taken, and the other left.

⁴¹ Two women shall be grinding at the mill; the one shall be taken, and the other left.

⁴² Watch therefore: for ye know not what hour your Lord doth come.

⁴³ But know this, that if the goodman of the house had known in what watch the thief would come, he would have watched, and would not have suffered his house to be broken up.

(Matthew 24:37-43)

It is amazing how people are busy in the world today, engaged in the affairs of this life. They are doing everything Jesus said would happen except expecting that the earth is actually coming to an end.

You see, the days of Noah and the days of Lot were two different dispensations and the writer of the gospels brought them together to make a statement that the same events will repeat. The problem with us - Christians, politicians, business men and women, religious people - is that we do not study history nor do we believe history.

Jesus warned that history would repeat itself. The Bible says the things that happened to them happened for our example that we may learn. But we are not learning; we are not studying history. We just live in our modern time and believe that we are good, that we are fine. We are neither good nor fine.

The reason people are very arrogant and treat people the way they do when they have money, political power, or some kind of exposure, connection, or relevance in society, is that they are not learning from history.

In the days of Noah, people went about their business as usual. There were no clouds so nobody listened to Noah. Today, God expects the church to warn the world of the Second Coming of Jesus and its implications for all men on earth. Unfortunately, the church is not sounding the trumpet of Christ's coming. We seem to be caught up in the ways of Noah's generation, exactly as Jesus warned.

Jesus is not saying that people should not marry and do business today. His concern is that we are so busy following the things of this life that we have put God on the bench. Some people have benched God for several years, yet they are engaged in so many things in which they need God's help.

3.
SIGNS OF THE END TIMES: THE APOSTLES' TEACHING

In Chapter 2, I focused on what Jesus Himself taught concerning the signs of the end times. Jesus laid the foundation for these teachings. In this chapter, I will focus on the early apostles' teaching on the topic. Toward the end of this chapter, I will give you the modern day version of these signs to complete the picture and bring clarity that we can run with in our day.

This is the graphic presentation the Apostle Paul wrote concerning the last days.

> 1 *This know also, that in the last days perilous times shall come.*
>
> 2 *For men shall be lovers of their own selves, covetous, boasters, proud, blasphemers, disobedient to parents, unthankful, unholy,*
>
> 3 *Without natural affection, trucebreakers, false accusers, incontinent, fierce, despisers of those that are good,*
>
> 4 *Traitors, heady, highminded, lovers of pleasures more than lovers of God;*

> Having a form of godliness, but denying the power thereof: from such turn away.
>
> 6 For of this sort are they which creep into houses, and lead captive silly women laden with sins, led away with divers lusts,
>
> 7 Ever learning, and never able to come to the knowledge of the truth.
>
> (2 Timothy 3:1-7)

Every honest person who is spiritual and very observant will have no doubts that Paul was right on target. This should not surprise anyone. You have to understand that Paul was writing not based on some human projections like the scientists, scholars, and the futurists of today; he wrote under the direct leading of the Holy Spirit, and that gives authenticity to what he wrote.

Try and refute that any of these are not happening today. If you are unable, then you understand my burden and the reality of the times we are in today.

LOVERS OF THEMSELVES

Check this one simple evidence of some people loving themselves more than loving God. They have stopped coming to church on Sunday morning because they are busy making money. God gave a simple command to us to gather in His house. When we come to church it is not to please the pastor; it is simple obedience to God's word. If you find something more important than being in God's presence, your commitment is questionable.

If people struggle with this simple instruction, can you imagine their response when God makes another demand of them, like to not marry an unbeliever who looks beautiful or who has a lot of money, or to not proceed with something they consider a potential money-making venture, which God knows is a death trap from the enemy?

> **When we follow this trend of behavior, we present a Christianity whose value system is weak, a system of beliefs where any of our convictions can be compromised at any time for anything that looks good.**

On Sunday morning, whether I am preaching or not, I will not meet you at the airport. I will see you after service, but not at the time for service. It does not matter what you are bringing to me, I will see you after church.

One of the signs of the end time is the spirit of Ananias and Saphirah. People will hold back what is due the house of God. They will give all kinds of excuses, justifying why they must hold back the portion that is due to God and, yet, they will give an impression as if they are big givers.

If you love God, you will give according to how He has blessed you to prove to God that you love Him. If you love God you will obey Him more than you obey man and the laws of the land. Today, people fear men more than they fear God and they are willing to disobey God and rather obey man who has no power to make their lives meaningful.

COVETOUS

Covetous people are never satisfied with what they have. They would like to have what others have as well, or at least in preference to what they have. If you look at somebody's spouse in a way that suggests you would have preferred her to your spouse that is covetousness.

You go to the car park and you see somebody's car. You stand by it and say, "Brother, we thank God for you. Your car is very nice." In your heart you are actually wishing you had a car like his; you are coveting his car.

One characteristic of covetous people is that they are never content. No matter what they have, they still want more or what they consider as better and will do anything to have what others have.

BOASTERS

Boasters show off. That is what it simply is. I am often reminded of the healing revival of Oral Roberts and a young man named Jack Cole. Cole had a healing ministry in those days. He was so powerful; he moved the cities. He packed the stadium. He became big and the media in those days started blowing him up so huge and this was what they did: they started calling him the evangelist of that time whose tent was bigger than that of Oral Roberts. He started building huge tents to compete with Oral Roberts. He died at the age of 38, and his ministry withered. Oral Roberts never said anything, and he lived more than 50 years after Cole. He died after 90 years, and his ministry is still alive and active today. It is a matter of time.

Today, there are preachers who are competing with other preachers. When it is time for them to build their churches, they don't build according to the grace upon them, like Paul would say. They want to build a church bigger than everyone else's.

What are you trying to prove, that you are the biggest in town? If you have the money to build, then build. But, don't build with the mindset that you want to prove a point. Some people build a church for 5,000 people and they say their congregation is 20,000. Why? Something is just wrong and nobody is addressing it.

I admonished a business friend about a situation in his country. I told him, "You are the reason for the mess in your country because you gave money to some of these young preachers who have not been tested and tried. Such preachers are empowered with money and through money they grow up overnight, competing with fathers, disrespecting and dishonoring fathers, and that is the reason for the mess going on in your country. Because they have money, they have no regard nor respect for elders and authority anymore."

Money does not mean anything. God has neither respect nor regard for your money. He has respect and regard for your love for Him, for your commitment to Him, and for your fear of Him.

Disobedient to Parents

I was talking to a parent the other day and she said, "My children are disobedient and I don't know what I haven't done. I've done everything right, raised them in the church, and I don't know what I've done wrong." I looked at her and said, "Don't worry about it. One of the signs of the end time is that children will be disobedient to their natural and spiritual parents. It is the spirit of the end time."

God commands children to obey their parents because parents are God's representatives on earth. There is no position you can rise to in this life that negates obedience to your parents. If you are a young man who has received good education from your parents, including studying abroad, which is considered an advantage, and you do not want your parents involved in the major decisions of your life, that is the spirit of disobedience.

The argument that children often put up is that it is their life and not their parents'. That is true, but how did they get to that point? Even if their parents played a minimal role in what they are today, the Bible still asks children to honor and obey their parents (Exo 20:12).

If your parents are not around, there is still a father figure you must learn to submit to because it is a spiritual principle. They cannot, for example, marry and call their parents and inform them that they just married. That is a violation of God's authority.

Can you marry without your father's blessing if he is still alive? You have to understand that you cannot go far in this life without the blessing. Blessing is what makes the difference. The Bible said that it is the blessing of the Lord that makes one rich, not his education.

UNTHANKFUL

We all remember in the earlier generations, if someone did something good for you, you thanked him immediately. Your parents would further demand that the following morning you went to the person and said "thank you" again. That was how much they practiced gratitude. It was one of the richest tenets of our culture as Africans.

The present generation of parents is struggling to teach their children this principle, and this simple act of saying "thank you" seems to be getting lost in the current generation. The frightening feature of this is that it is eating into the youth of the church today.

I expect my children to appreciate what I do for them because, although I am doing it out of love, it is just nice and Godly when they say, "Thank you, Daddy."

The sense of gratitude is getting lost, and I want to speak to the young foundation. Learn to say "thank you" to your parents. Today, children come from school and their parents are with a guest in their sitting room and the children don't even know how to stop and greet their parent and the guest. The just walk to their room on their cell phone; they are chatting. Something is wrong with this generation.

The attitude of thanksgiving is waning in our society. People seem to be moving away from saying "thank you" in all sincerity. There is no gratitude in the church, even toward God. God does things for us and we don't even say "Thank you".

There is no testimony in the church anymore because it does not matter what God does for us. We don't give testimony in the church anymore because people feel they are entitled to success and that God is under obligation to bless them. That is how far we have deviated, and it is a matter of serious concern.

Nevertheless, giving testimony is glorifying God and showing gratitude to God for what He has done.

WITHOUT NATURAL AFFECTION

The competition to be ahead of everyone is killing the natural affection toward each other as the family of God. People seem to not care about others. Sometimes they choose whom to show affection toward and forget everyone else.

If you are in church and you see that the person sitting by you wears the same shoes every Sunday, and you have many shoes but won't give them any, that is selfishness and lack of care. They wear the same clothes and you have many but won't share. That is another manifestation of the lack of affection; no sensitivity; no compassion; no one cares about anyone else.

You have to understand and accept that the church is not a lecture hall where you come with your notebook, receive lectures, and go back home. The church is a family, the family of God; and we have to care for one another. When God blesses you with a car, which I see all the time in my church, and you think it is for you and your spouse and children alone, you miss the point. The car is for the brethren. After service, people stand by the roadside and you don't give anyone a ride, even halfway. It shows that you don't understand the principle here.

When I got born again there was an old man who used to help me in the things of God. He's now in heaven. Every now and then some of his children and relatives will call me. Sometimes they do so at very odd hours and it becomes a bother. I cautioned one of them about it but he kept doing it, so I considered changing my number. But God said to me, "Son, after everything their father did for you, you can't just endure a little bother from his son calling you at odd hours, because you are a very important person now? You are going to change your telephone number? Can't you go out of your way to do something for them?" I repented that very moment and sent them something.

Sometimes we don't want to endure a little annoyance. Longsuffering is also giving way in the church. We have become so principled and sophisticated that if somebody bothers us a little, we decide to stop attending church.

Some of you don't even want anyone to visit you in your house. Somebody comes to your house, and you ask, "What do you want in my house?" You are offended that the Christian brothers who pass by decided to check on you. I know that there are some who come around to trouble you. I know that, but don't put everybody in the same category.

LOVERS OF PLEASURE MORE THAN LOVERS OF GOD

People in this category focus more on themselves than on God. They put their vacation, their acquisition of property, the time they spend with their playmates, etc., above the house of God and God's people. It is always about them and never about God nor the house of God, nor God's people.

Some time ago, someone brought me a gift that I wasn't praying for. I did not need it. As soon as he brought it, I started making plans for it and the Lord said to me, "It is not yours. Don't touch it. Put it down. I'm using you to answer somebody's prayers." Just then my office called and said there was a lady downstairs, a single mother, who wanted to see me. I asked what the matter was, but they did not know, but said it looked as if she was very troubled. I asked that she be sent up to my office.

My mother was a single mother when she was raising me up so I really have a soft spot for them. The lady came up and was crying. She did not have money for her children's fees, could not pay her rent, and things were bad for her. So, I asked her how much she would need. She mentioned the very amount that was brought to me so I took that envelope and gave it to her. She couldn't believe it. She thanked and thanked me, blessing me and crying. But, you know something? I was so blessed that I could be a blessing to somebody. That is what Christianity is all about.

Do you know how people bring curses on themselves? You see, that envelope that was brought to me was not mine. God said, "I'm using you to answer somebody's prayers." This is the mistake in the church and this is spiritual corruption. Somebody will cry, and fast and pray and God will answer their prayer by bringing you the answer to their prayer; and then, because of selfishness and greed, you use it for yourself and the person's needs are not met. Then they go back, crying and praying to God, and God says, "But I've answered your prayer," and they're still crying. If you do that you bring a curse upon yourself.

Those of you who hoard, you hold back the tithes, you hold back the first fruit, you hold back things because you don't want people to know you're blessed. You are playing games with God. God knows everything about you and He is blessing you so that tithe can come into the church and bless others, but you hold it back. That is why the Bible says you are cursed with a curse.

DEPARTURES FROM THE FAITH

> ¹ *Now the Spirit speaketh expressly, that in the latter times some shall depart from the faith, giving heed to seducing spirits, and doctrines of devils;*
>
> ² *Speaking lies in hypocrisy; having their conscience seared with a hot iron;*
>
> *(1 Timothy 4:1-2)*

Many are departing from the faith. I started preaching at the age of 20 and have been preaching for 41 years by God's grace, and I've seen many fall from the faith. It breaks my heart, but what can I do? The best I can do is to love and encourage them, speak the Word to them, and pray for them, and trust that they come back.

If you see what some believers do today, the kinds of places they go will shock you. Some even go to the cemetery to unveil tombs and work all kinds of divinations. Some may argue that Mary Magdalene went to the tomb to anoint Jesus. What they don't factor in is that she did not go to consult the dead; she went to embalm the dead body. That is the belief of the

Jews and not a New Testament biblical doctrine. If any pastor talks about going to the cemetery for spiritual reasons, abandon him altogether and save your soul.

You have to be careful when it comes to loved ones who are dead. In this part of the world, people worship the dead and engage them in all kinds of beliefs. These are all doctrines of devils. The Bible says that for the believer, absent in the flesh means present with the Lord. We have no dealings with the dead.

One pastor said, "If you want people to paint your house, pretend that you are dead." It is true. I've seen people spend so much money on the dead. We celebrate the dead in this country, and if the money we spend on the dead were spent on them while alive, they would live longer. We have value for the dead, paying what is called last respect. That is all hypocrisy.

4.
WHAT OCCUPIES YOU TODAY?

¹ *If ye then be risen with Christ, seek those things which are above, where Christ sitteth on the right hand of God.*

² *Set your affection on things above, not on things on the earth.*

³ *For ye are dead, and your life is hid with Christ in God.*

⁴ *When Christ, who is our life, shall appear, then shall ye also appear with him in glory.*

(Colossians 3:1-4)

If we accept that the Second Coming of Jesus is not a myth but reality; if we accept that we are living in the last days and Christ's coming is closer than when we first believed as per the many signs of the end times; then we should be asking ourselves the all-important question: What are we doing as we look forward to that great event?

WHERE IS YOUR MIND?

The Apostle Paul's writing to the church in Colossae makes life easier for us by prompting us with the above passage. His message is simple: Set your mind on the things above, not on things on the earth.

He continued to remind us that our lives are hidden in Christ and that He is coming back with our new lives that will be revealed at His coming. This is a deep spiritual truth that has a lot of positive implications even for our lives as we wait for the great day.

Let me take you back to the warning Jesus gave as cited earlier on in this book. Jesus said that the coming of the Lord would be like in the days of Noah and like in the days of Sodom and Gomorrah. What were those days? Those were days of business as usual. They were marrying, building houses, and purchasing lands; everything that man does now was happening then. They were drinking, partying, having a good time, and making deals. Jesus did not imply that men should not do all these things; He was denoting that, in the process of doing these things, men should be 100% conscious of eternity.

This world continues to bombard us with so many things – the good, the bad, and the ugly. It has become the order of the day to the extent that we often forget we are in transit and that this is not our final destination. Sometimes you can be in transit and go to a town and you love the place and admire everything there, but you can't stay there because it is not your final destination. You are just passing through.

If you're going to China and you stop over in Dubai for a few days, you don't live in Dubai as if that is your final destination, because it is not.

My assignment is to equip you and bring you to the awareness and understanding that you and I are in transit and this is not our final destination. We should, therefore, never forget ourselves and allow the success and the beauties of the transit location capture our entire being. We stand the danger of being derailed from continuing our journey to our destination, as is actually happening to many Christians today.

We came from somewhere. We are here for a reason and we shall return and give an account of what we did here with the life, the resources, and the time that was given to us.

The enemy has succeeded in bewitching us and making us forget why we are here. The result is that we are living carelessly and walking aimlessly. But we need to live soberly, watchfully. We need to live with the understanding that even if we live 100 or 1,000 years, this is not our final destination.

Years ago, the church was mocked as being so heavenly minded that we were of no earthly use. Those were the times when the average believer was conscious of righteous living, of soul winning, and of Christian values. Those were times when heaven was our thinking. It showed in the songs we composed and sang, and in all the stories we told.

Today the picture is different. It can well be said of the church that we are becoming so earthly minded that we are of no heavenly use. Granting that those are two evils, which would you choose?

> **Would you rather be mocked as a heaven fanatic, or be hailed as a lover of the world? Each man decides for himself and becomes responsible for his choice.**

WHERE IS YOUR TREASURE?

Jesus made a profound statement worth considering here:

> [19] *Lay not up for yourselves treasures upon earth, where moth and rust doth corrupt, and where thieves break through and steal:*
>
> [20] *But lay up for yourselves treasures in heaven, where neither moth nor rust doth corrupt, and where thieves do not break through nor steal:*
>
> [21] *For where your treasure is, there will your heart be also.*

(Matthew 6:19-21)

This is one of the statements Jesus made that affirms His commitment to heaven. Jesus constantly made statements to let us know and understand that heaven is far more a reality than the earth as we have it now. Jesus implies that no amount of achievements we make on earth can negate heaven nor make heaven second-class.

If you project that statement further, it comes up to having heaven in mind in all you do while on earth. Look at the analogy Jesus makes here. He says whatever you store on earth you are storing for moth and rust to destroy; not so with the things you store in heaven.

It is clear that many Christians today are busy storing things here on earth. Their lives consist of how much property remains here in their name – houses, cars, businesses, money stored in accounts, gold and precious metals held in banks, etc.

Many have their net worth calculated in earthly terms, not in heavenly terms. Jesus' statement, *"For what shall it profit a man, if he shall gain the whole world, and lose his own soul"* (Mark 8:36)?

Is that not part of the thinking of the ordinary Christian today. We are chasing the wind. We are following the empty promises of technology and the vain pleasures of humanistic ideologies that are questioning established Bible traditions. We are actually digging a grave that we will eventually fall in, all because we have not taken heed to any of Jesus' words.

Beware of a Glittering World

Perhaps this is a good time to throw in a common saying: "All that glitters is not gold."

Man is making a lot of progress when it comes to making life easier. Technology seems to take away the difficulties that existed yesterday. As a preacher, you don't have to strain your voice to speak to a crowd gathered at the Independence Square in my country.

I don't have to travel to every part of the world physically for my messages to be heard worldwide. I could continue this list. We all know, however, that what technology cannot do is change the human heart. It actually reveals the evil in the human heart.

The world system orchestrated and operated by Satan and his demons have taken advantage of technology, bringing out the evil in man more to the world than before. Because of the loudness of their voice, the voice of conscience seems to be faint. The wrong is hailed as right and the right is frowned and looked down upon. That is the world's system.

What is the Apostle John teaching us about our attitude to the world, especially in a time when Jesus is calling us to be heavenly-minded and set our treasures in heaven and not on earth?

> 15 Do not love the world or the things in the world. If anyone loves the world, the love of the Father is not in him.
>
> 16 For all that is in the world—the desires of the flesh and the desires of the eyes and pride of life—is not from the Father but is from the world
>
> 17 And the world is passing away along with its desires, but whoever does the will of God abides forever.
>
> (1 John 2:15-17)

If you want to abide forever, in other words, have a part in God's eternity when Jesus comes back, you should be paying more heed to John's teaching than you have before. Remember that these were the men who walked with, touched [handled], saw with their eyes, and heard the Savior and Lord when He walked on our earth.

WHERE'S YOUR CHRISTIAN COMMITMENT?

Ask yourself, "What have I contributed to the church?" Have you contributed one chair to the chairs we sit on? Do you have a pillar in the house of God? Have you saved a soul since the beginning of the year that you can say, "God, I am the reason why this individual is born again? This is my fruit; this is my contribution to the kingdom." What is your value? What is your use? Why should God be happy with you?

Sometimes people come into my office and say, "Papa, please pray for me. I need God to intervene for me."

Then I ask them a few questions. "Do you tithe? Are you involved in any church activities? Do you attend cell meetings? What do you do in the church?"

Often these people are doing nothing in church.

We need to take stock. We need to look at our lives and see where we stand with God. So many don't attend home cells because they look at the people who go to the home cells and they are not people of their caliber. You look at yourself and say, "I am a CEO. I live in a marble and granite house and can't allow cells in my house because people will come in there with all kinds of shoes and dirty up the place."

If you feel your cars belong to you only, so you don't give anybody a ride, you are already in violation of the spiritual law of sharing. You are not going anywhere with it. You will leave them all here and they don't give you any mileage in heaven, and it means nothing to God.

Such scenarios break my spirit and suddenly I lose the unction to function. Suddenly, I lose the anointing and disconnect from the radars of eternity, the frequencies of heaven. I don't even know where to begin and where to end.

What's the reason? All of a sudden I find myself standing and looking at a selfish individual, one who appears to be taking advantage of God, exploiting the kingdom for personal reasons. This I call, "spiritual corruption."

My assignment is to remind you that we all came to this life for a purpose and we will answer to Him one day, whether we fulfilled it or not.

5.
WHERE IS YOUR SOUL-WINNING FIRE?

> *And this gospel of the kingdom shall be preached in all the world for a witness unto all nations; and then shall the end come.*
>
> *(Matthew 24:14)*

In the previous chapter, I drew your attention to heavenly-mindedness and the need for us to lay up treasures in heaven and not on earth. In this chapter, I want to highlight one of the greatest ways we can be sure we are laying treasures in heaven.

Let's start with this argument. What is it you have in your hand that you want to present to God when you meet Him one day when life on earth is over? Certainly not the number of houses you built on earth. The last time I checked, all these will melt with fervent heat.

Don't even think of your bank accounts stored in digital form. Guess, all the cyber capacity will give way to God's new system of communication!

> *But the day of the Lord will come like a thief, and then the heavens will pass away with a*

roar, and the heavenly bodies will be burned up and dissolved, and the earth and the works that are done on it will be exposed

(2 Peter 3:10)

Everything we see and cherish today will be burned up and will give way. None of them have a lasting capacity. It is only a matter of time!

JESUS ON WINNING THE LOST

In the parable of the lost sheep, Jesus made a profound statement.

> 3 And he spake this parable unto them, saying,
>
> 4 What man of you, having an hundred sheep, if he lose one of them, doth not leave the ninety and nine in the wilderness, and go after that which is lost, until he find it?
>
> 5 And when he hath found it, he layeth it on his shoulders, rejoicing.
>
> 6 And when he cometh home, he calleth together his friends and neighbours, saying unto them, Rejoice with me; for I have found my sheep which was lost.

⁷ *I say unto you, that likewise joy shall be in heaven over one sinner that repenteth, more than over ninety and nine just persons, which need no repentance.*

(Luke 15:3-7)

The question each of us must be asking is this: When was the last time you kept the angels rejoicing? You can ask it another way: How many times since I became a Christian have I caused rejoicing to take place in heaven?

This is a question for pastors, bishops, and whatever title or position you hold in the body of Christ. Your life is either directly or indirectly bringing someone from the kingdom of darkness into the kingdom of light or it is not! That is what it finally comes up to.

Some are busy today telling Christians how they can have money and compete with the unbelievers. There is Scripture that we can quote to support that agenda. *Our heavenly Father owns everything so if the people of the world are flying in their private jets, why should we not?* I have heard all those arguments, but in all these, we are producing Christians who don't know how to share the gospel with an unbeliever. In fact, we are producing Christians who don't have the slightest urge to actively share their faith in Christ.

> **The gospel is not that Jesus will make you financially prosperous. It is that Jesus will save you from your sin, make you God's child, transform your life, and prepare you for eternity.**

If you got born again in the 1970s or thereabout, you can testify to the fire in our hearts to share the gospel. We shared the gospel in buses, trotro, taxis, street corners, houses, and everywhere we found ourselves. Our message was that Jesus is coming again to take home His own – all who believe in Him.

We had dawn broadcasts and rural evangelism, visited hospitals and prisons, and shared the gospel with people. We were more interested in people becoming Christians than becoming rich. That is sometimes often misunderstood that the church in those days endorsed poverty and shun prosperity. We were so full of the consciousness of heaven and getting heaven populated as hell is depopulated.

What has Happened to that Fire?

I am sure that if God speaks to the church today, He will be telling us what He told the angel to tell the church in Ephesus

> ² I know your works, your toil and your patient endurance, and how you cannot bear with those who are evil, but have tested those who call themselves apostles and are not, and found them to be false.
>
> ³ I know you are enduring patiently and bearing up for my name's sake, and you have not grown weary.
>
> ⁴ But I have this against you, that you have abandoned the love you had at first.
>
> ⁵ Remember therefore from where you have fallen; repent, and do the works you did at first. If not, I will come to you and remove your lampstand from its place, unless you repent
>
> (Revelation 2:2-5)

What happened to the bubbling in our hearts to tell people the gospel and invite them to come to Jesus? That, to me, is the greatest service we can render to humanity. The people of the world are applying the principles of success and prosperity in their businesses and they are succeeding financially.

We know that they are not going to heaven when they leave here. Why do we continue to hail them and make them feel good, especially those that give fat offerings to the church but their hearts are far away from God?

When was the last time you spoke to someone about the implications of living their lives without Christ, and gave them the opportunity to give their life to Christ?

If you are a pastor, ask yourself the last time you taught your congregation the gospel in its entirety that will help your congregation witness for Christ? What programs and activities do you have in your church that challenge and provide opportunity to the youth, for example, to win their own to Christ? There are elderly folks in your church, how are you mobilizing them to share the gospel with the younger generation as they wait to transition to eternity?

Examine your preaching Sunday after Sunday and ask if sinners will truly be saved when they come to your church, or if they will be looking to become rich and prosperous. Is it not time we let the sacrificial work of Christ by His shed blood play center stage in our messages regardless of what we teach on Sunday?

When was the last time this song below was sung in your congregation? How many of your congregants even know there is a song like that?

> *Rescue the perishing, care for the dying,*
> *Snatch them in pity from sin and the grave;*
> *Weep o'er the erring one, lift up the fallen,*
> *Tell them of Jesus, the mighty to save.*

Refrain:
Rescue the perishing, care for the dying,
Jesus is merciful, Jesus will save.

Though they are slighting Him, still He is waiting,
Waiting the penitent child to receive;
Plead with them earnestly, plead with them gently;
He will forgive if they only believe.

Down in the human heart, crushed by the tempter,
Feelings lie buried that grace can restore;
Touched by a loving heart, wakened by kindness,
Chords that were broken will vibrate once more.

Rescue the perishing, duty demands it;
Strength for thy labor the Lord will provide;
Back to the narrow way patiently win them;
Tell the poor wand'rer a Savior has died.

(Lyrics by Fanny Jane Crosby, 1820-1915)

I am sure the youth in your congregation know all the songs of Nathaniel Bassey, Israel Houghton, of Sinach, of Ohemaa Mercy and Joe Mettle and all, except the ones that challenge people to never rest until heaven is being populated and hell depopulated.

Songs like *Rescue the Perishing* makes real the urgency of saving souls for the kingdom. If we must go back to our first love, we must certainly go back to evangelizing the lost world, telling them of the love of Jesus.

Regarding those who constantly refuse, we help them understand the danger that awaits all who intentionally reject God. There is no other way to get this done but by being intentional and proactive about it.

> **Evangelism does not happen if we don't make it happen. People will not open their hearts to the Savior if they don't get the exact picture of life after death.**

We must guard against numerous people coming to our services because we provide good music and make the place very friendly, and yet they are not born again. The greatest tragedy is having a large percentage of your congregants not born again while you sit on TV and talk about how great your ministry is and how God is expanding your infrastructure and your facilities.

Check the true statistics of your church and ascertain how many people in your church are your converts and not people who migrated from another church because you talked about faith and how faith can give them more money. We cannot recycle members and make noise about it while thousands live a life without Christ.

People think the church is dead. The church of Jesus Christ is not growing like it should grow. It is transferred growth. People are not saving the lost anymore. We are targeting people in established Bible believing churches and inviting them to our church. There are churches that literally work to compel their people to bring believers from other churches.

There are so many people who don't go to church on Sunday morning, but we don't go out for them. We are looking for believers. There are believers who have sat down in churches, grown in the church, but because of offense they leave their church and take some more believers with them. The Bible calls such work of iniquity, destroying the kingdom. You cannot scatter what God is building, and yet believe that Jesus is your Lord. You can't do that.

Christians of today are not winning souls anymore. It is common to find pastors poaching people who are well to do financially, and poach them to participate in their programs. In the process they invite them to join their churches, quickly give them recognition and they become key members in their churches. Soul winning is not getting people who are already born again and established in churches to become your members.

> **If you increase your church membership by luring Christians from other churches to become your members, you cannot call that church growth. The church today is actually recycling members, not winning fresh souls.**

Church growth is when we go out there and win the souls who don't know Jesus, are not born again, and don't go to church on Sunday, and lead them to Christ. Then you bring them in, baptize them in water and in the Holy Ghost, and groom them in the things of God. That is soul winning.

Let's go back to winning the lost for the kingdom of God. That is our highest service while on earth today.

6.
READY FOR FLIGHT H-E-A-V-E-N?

> ²⁵ *Husbands, love your wives, even as Christ also loved the church, and gave himself for it;*
>
> ²⁶ *That he might sanctify and cleanse it with the washing of water by the word,*
>
> ²⁷ *That he might present it to himself a glorious church, not having spot, or wrinkle, or any such thing; but that it should be holy and without blemish.*
>
> *(Ephesians 5:25-27)*

The passage above is usually cited when pastors are officiating weddings. Look again at the analogy Jesus is making. It immediately has an instruction for husbands, but it has much more than that. It is saying more about Christ and His church.

Jesus loves the church so much. His goal is to present a church that is blameless and without spot to the heavenly Father. What it means is that Jesus expects each of us who have believed in Him to become pure and blameless. Don't get scared by that because it is possible. If it were not possible, Jesus would not have made that His ultimate goal.

How does the purity of the church fit into the whole event like the Second Coming of Jesus Christ? It becomes clear if you understand how the rapture will happen. We know that in principle the rapture will separate saints from sinners on earth, but let's look at the act itself. This is the Apostle Paul's writing:

> [13] But I would not have you to be ignorant, brethren, concerning them which are asleep, that ye sorrow not, even as others which have no hope.
>
> [14] For if we believe that Jesus died and rose again, even so them also which sleep in Jesus will God bring with him.
>
> [15] For this we say unto you by the word of the Lord, that we which are alive and remain unto the coming of the Lord shall not prevent them which are asleep.
>
> [16] For the Lord himself shall descend from heaven with a shout, with the voice of the archangel, and with the trump of God: and the dead in Christ shall rise first:
>
> [17] Then we which are alive and remain shall be caught up together with them in the clouds, to meet the Lord in the air: and so shall we ever be with the Lord.
>
> (1 Thessalonians 4:13-17)

The above passage from Apostle Paul's letter to the church in Thessalonica gives us a glimpse of how the believers will be raptured when Jesus comes. You have to understand that this is a spiritual event.

In other words, God's Spirit is going to pull first the believers who died before this event; then we who are alive will be pulled up. This pulling is a spirit-by-spirit occurrence. It is not a work of the flesh.

Spiritual Magnetism

When studying magnetism in your physics class, you are told that opposite poles attract and like poles repel. An example of like poles attracting is when you bring a magnet close to an object, that object must have some properties similar to the magnet before they can be pulled by the magnet. That explains why a magnet can pull iron filings or the paper clips in your office or the metal spoon in your house, and not the plastic cup you have at home.

Plastic, wood, paper, etc. have nothing in common with a magnet so no matter what you do, the magnet cannot pull them unto itself. As a matter of fact, if you put them on the magnet, they will fall off.

What is it that you and the Spirit of God have in common? The first is that God is spirit, and you also have a spirit.

We can say you are spirit living in a human body for that matter, so you and God have that in common.

The second thing that is critical is that the Spirit of God abides in you if you are a believer. That is God's promise from the Old Testament that was fulfilled in the New Testament.

The critical factor here is that God's Spirit is holy and pure. That is why we call Him the Holy Spirit. It is not just His name; it is His identity.

This means that for this pulling to happen at the rapture, you must also have purity in your spirit. If you have been baptized with the Holy Spirit and you speak, pray, and sing in tongues then you should be holy. Why do we often separate the two?

> **It is a tragedy to find people who speak, sing, and pray in tongues for hours and still are not living holy. It is difficult to explain that, but it certainly is a serious phenomenon that needs urgent correction.**

Have you thought about what could happen if you do not have purity in your spirit at the time Jesus touches down? God's Holy Spirit must find holiness in you the believer before the pulling [catching up] can take place. You have to understand this event and the phenomenon very well. It means that if there is darkness somewhere, the pulling cannot take place. Light must pull only light to itself in this equation, as explained earlier.

That is what the apostle John communicates to the church when he wrote in 1 John 3:1-3:

> [1] Behold, what manner of love the Father hath bestowed upon us, that we should be called the sons of God: therefore the world knows us not, because it knew him not.
>
> [2] Beloved, now are we the sons of God, and it doth not yet appear what we shall be: but we know that, when he shall appear, we shall be like him; for we shall see him as he is.
>
> [3] And every man that hath this hope in him purifies himself, even as he is pure.
>
> (I John 3:1-3)

Note that this passage is also in connection with the Second Coming of Jesus Christ. He teaches that we shall be like Him. That means we shall look like Him. That is what it takes to live in His heaven where there is no blemish. There is no sin and no darkness in heaven and we have to be pure to be able to live there.

That introduces the number one component of the readiness agenda: live a life of holiness.

Work Out your Own Salvation

We start our Christian life by being born again. At new birth our sins are forgiven because the blood of Jesus Christ cleanses them. There is no substitute to this. Only with the blood is atonement made for sins.

With our sins forgiven, however, the path that lies ahead of us is a process by which the sin nature in us is dealt with through several processes that God has predetermined. From the new birth to being taken up when Jesus comes, we go through a period of refinement. Our sin nature is subjected to the power of the Holy Spirit for the purpose of our transformation.

The Apostle Paul, in the following verses, describes the transformation process that gets the believer to the point that he is ready to be pulled by the Spirit of God:

> [12] *Wherefore, my beloved, as ye have always obeyed, not as in my presence only, but now much more in my absence, work out your own salvation with fear and trembling.*

¹³ *For it is God which works in you both to will and to do of his good pleasure.*

¹⁴ *Do all things without murmurings and disputings:*

¹⁵ *That ye may be blameless and harmless, the sons of God, without rebuke, in the midst of a crooked and perverse nation, among whom ye shine as lights in the world;*

(Philippians 2:12-15)

The same Apostle Paul who wrote that "salvation" is a gift, not of works, is the same who wrote the passage above. It then becomes clear that the word "salvation" means two different things in different contexts.

The first context relates to being accepted by God by virtue of the atoning death of Jesus Christ on the cross by which His blood was shed for the entire humanity.

The second context relates to dealing with the sinful nature of man to make him pure. The writer of Hebrews teaches us that without holiness no man can see God.

¹² *Therefore strengthen the hands which hang down, and the feeble knees,*

¹³ *and make straight paths for your feet, so that what is lame may not be dislocated, but rather be healed.*

> ¹⁴ *Pursue peace with all people, and holiness, without which no one will see the Lord:*
>
> ¹⁵ *looking carefully lest anyone fall short of the grace of God; lest any root of bitterness springing up cause trouble, and by this many become defiled;*
>
> *(Hebrews 12:12-15)*

SANCTIFICATION

The second interpretation of the word "salvation" given by theologians is sanctification. This has to do with what we go through to eventually look like Jesus Christ our Lord. Here are some verses speaking about the progressive nature of our Christian lives as it relates to sanctification.

> ¹ *I beseech you therefore, brethren, by the mercies of God, that ye present your bodies a living sacrifice, holy, acceptable unto God, which is your reasonable service.*
>
> ² *And be not conformed to this world: but be ye transformed by the renewing of your mind, that ye may prove what is that good, and acceptable, and perfect, will of God.*
>
> *(Romans 12:1-2)*

> *I am crucified with Christ: nevertheless I live; yet not I, but Christ liveth in me: and the life which I now live in the flesh I live by the faith of the Son of God, who loved me, and gave himself for me.*
>
> *(Galatians 2:20)*
>
> *For this is the will of God, even your sanctification, that ye should abstain from fornication:*
>
> *(1 Thessalonians 4:3)*

Listen to what Jesus Himself said:

> *And for their sakes I sanctify Myself, that they also may be sanctified by the truth.*
>
> *(John 17:19)*

The topic of sanctification is not now preached in the church anymore because, for whatever reason, we think that when you talk about sanctification it means you are a sinner or doing something wrong. That is not the point. It is necessary and it is critical that we talk about the subject of sanctification.

The Bible said that Jesus was tempted at every point that you and I are tempted, but yet He was without sin. The Man that was without sin said "And for their sakes I sanctify myself, that they also might be sanctified through the truth"

(John 17:19). So, if Jesus was without sin and He had to sanctify Himself, what is He trying to convey to us?

The immediate conclusion we can draw is that sanctification is a lifestyle. To be sanctified is to set your life apart. In the Old Testament a lot is said about the Nazarites. They were set apart unto God. In other words, they were separated unto God. The implications are critical. There are things that everyone else could do but a Nazarene could not do.

Sampson, for example, was not to go near a dead body, drink wine, or cut his hair. Today we have funerals all over the place and people attend them. They drink, and there are some pastors who would like to have no hair on their head so they shave.

The point here is that those things the Nazarites were forbidden are to single them out. It is a symbol of being singled out for God for a purpose. Yes, the believer has been called out and set apart for a purpose. Here is what the Apostle Peter wrote:

> [9] *But ye are a chosen generation, a royal priesthood, an holy nation, a peculiar people; that ye should show forth the praises of him who hath called you out of darkness into his marvelous light;*

> [10] *Which in time past were not a people, but are now the people of God: which had not obtained mercy, but now have obtained mercy.*
>
> [11] *Dearly beloved, I beseech you as strangers and pilgrims, abstain from fleshly lusts, which war against the soul;*
>
> (1 Peter 2:9-11)

The Bible calls us a peculiar people. It means that we are different from the rest of humanity. We are more than Nazarites in our generation. We are to show forth the praises of God who has called us out of darkness.

> **The command to show forth the praises of Him who called us out of darkness is not a call to sing "worship songs" and tell people our God is greater than all, and the like. We show forth the praises of our God by the Christ-like lives we lead.**

Jesus said that men should see our good works and declare the glory of God. It is not your singing that constitutes praise. It is your life that is challenging some unbeliever in your community to open his mouth and say, "His God is the God that all should worship." That is what the Apostle Peter communicates by this passage. We have been set apart to glorify God everywhere we go.

Working out your salvation involves being influenced by the Word of God; being governed by the Word; being guided by Scripture; and letting Scripture determine your choices and your decision and your lifestyle. Let Scripture have preeminence in your thought patterns. Your upbringing, your culture, your tradition, your educational background, your brilliance and your intelligence, all mean nothing without the influence of Scripture.

Daily sanctification is living a spirit-driven life, a spirit-controlled life, a spirit-inspired life, a spirit-filled life, a spirit-convicted life, a spirit-led life, and a spirit-dying life.

It means not living by your own feelings or dictates of the flesh, but being driven by the Holy Ghost, and staying sanctified on a daily basis. It is daily sanctification, watchfulness, vigilance, soberness, and diligence that guarantees you will enter into the kingdom when Jesus comes. You can see the kingdom and not enter if you take living a sanctified life for granted.

Sanctification involves transformation. The Apostle Paul added his voice to make this point clearer to us when he wrote to the church in Rome.

> *And do not be conformed to this world, but be transformed by the renewing of your mind, that you may prove what is that good and acceptable and perfect will of God.*
>
> *(Romans 12:2)*

It is not enough to be born again and remain conformed to this world, as is the case with some. It is dangerous. You cannot claim to be born again and live and think and act like an unbeliever and like a heathen. If you are not transformed, you can come to church on Sunday, and then on Monday be on the highway cursing, insulting, and fighting people. You cannot go to work and fight your boss and don't greet your colleagues; fight your siblings; or act like an unsaved person, living by your flesh and your feelings, and emotions. That does not describe someone wanting to be pulled by God's Spirit when the rapture comes.

You will never know the good, the acceptable, and the perfect will of God after you are born again if you are not renewing your mind. If you think you are born again and still act like an unbeliever, the danger is that you may not enter the kingdom with that kind of a lifestyle. That is not a sanctified life.

BEWARE OF SEXUAL IMMORALITY

One major work of the flesh that is destroying many Christian lives is the sin of fornication. We know there are no small sins and big sins, but we know the trauma people go through if they commit fornication or adultery and it comes to light. Even when it has not come to light, they live in the fear of the possibility of this coming out in the light. It is a terrible sin. The Apostle Paul explained why sexual immorality is terrible when he wrote to the church at Corinth to flee fornication.

> [18] Flee fornication. Every sin that a man doeth is without the body, but he that commits fornication sins against his own body.
>
> [19] What? know ye not that your body is the temple of the Holy Ghost which is in you, which ye have of God, and ye are not your own?
>
> [20] For ye are bought with a price: therefore glorify God in your body, and in your spirit, which are God's.
>
> (1 Corinthians 6:18-20)

This sin defiles the temple of God, which you are since you became born again. If God convicts you and you continue in this sin, there comes a time when He decides you have had enough. What happens after that point is in His sovereign hands.

We need to pray for our youth because of the kind of world they live in today. Sex has been presented as a game, like children play with toys. Truly, women have been presented like toys to play with and throw away when you feel like. Hollywood has not helped this generation. It spends billions of dollars every year to promote uncontrolled, unlimited sex at all levels, in all kinds of forms, and under all kinds of conditions.

The world has destroyed the sanctity that God created sex to be. Sexual perversion is all over our screens morning, noon, and night. Young people today have access to nudity on their phones and in the media everywhere.

People today no longer think of sex as partnership with God to procreate and bring people into the world. Such understanding would have communicated the idea of sex as something very sacred and holy, and people would think twice before getting involved.

The church has not helped much in this either. Sometimes the way we present marriage to the young people creates the impression that marriage is the opportunity for them to also have sex. No wonder many youth today cannot wait to get married before having sex because marriage looks far away for them. We are not teaching them the values of abstinence, and that God can help them abstain from pre-marital sex.

Apart from the youth, we have to pray against the rate of adultery reported in the church today. It is eating up many lives and we cannot merely criticize and complain. We need to launch a spiritual attack to break down its fortifications and foundations in every member of our congregations. We have to keep our bodies holy unto the Lord.

The church must rise up in prayer and battle this evil, as the coming of the Lord is closer than before. We should not stop preaching, teaching, and helping our congregants walk in purity. It has proven itself to be a major challenge. It starts by living pure ourselves, as pastors, living above reproach when it comes to matters of sexuality.

Jesus is coming for a church without blemish and we should be that church.

> [24] *And let us consider one another to provoke unto love and to good works:*
>
> [25] *Not forsaking the assembling of ourselves together, as the manner of some is; but exhorting one another: and so much the more, as ye see the day approaching.*

(Hebrews 10:24-25)

And now, little children, abide in him; that, when he shall appear, we may have confidence, and not be ashamed before him at his coming.

(1 John 2:28)

7.
Don't be left Behind

> ³⁴ I tell you, in that night there shall be two men in one bed; the one shall be taken, and the other shall be left.
>
> ³⁵ Two women shall be grinding together; the one shall be taken, and the other left.
>
> ³⁶ Two men shall be in the field; the one shall be taken, and the other left.
>
> ³⁷ And they answered and said unto him, Where, Lord? And he said unto them, Wheresover the body is, thither will the eagles be gathered together.
>
> (Luke 17:34-37)

I want to start this chapter with the reaffirmation of the Second Coming of Jesus Christ. The earlier affirmations I presented were in the gospels. Those were statements Jesus made when He was living on earth like one of us. Those were statements of the Word made flesh and dwelling amongst us.

These latter affirmations are from the King of kings and the Lord of lords who sits on the throne with 24 elders and thousands and tens of thousands of angels worshipping Him daily.

He which testifieth these things saith, Surely I come quickly. Amen. Even so, come, Lord Jesus.

(Revelation 22:20)

And, behold, I come quickly; and my reward is with me, to give every man according as his work shall be.

(Revelation 22:12)

Behold, I come quickly: hold that fast which thou hast, that no man take thy crown.

(Revelation 3:11)

Let the above verses settle any doubt in your mind concerning the Second Coming of Jesus. It is certainly the most glorious event of human history following Christmas and Easter. Christmas heralded the Word becoming flesh so we can behold our heavenly Father. Easter sealed access for us into the family of God by sacrificial death and atoning blood. The Second Coming ensures that we are removed totally from the presence of sin and its effects forever and ever, Amen!

Before He left the earth by ascension, Jesus taught truths that will help each of us book our place on the flight to H-E-A-V-E-N. Principally, what He taught was to ensure that no one would be left behind. The first of those that I want to present here is below.

The passage in Luke 17 cited above is one of the passages that look very frightening, and no other person than Jesus Himself made it. It establishes that not all who think they will be caught up will actually be caught up. It also sends the alert that each one must make sure he has a place on the flight. It is not a mystery that some will be picked up and some will be left. It will happen that way because some followed God's ways and others did not.

Jesus spoke a parable about ten virgins who were invited to a wedding banquet. For some reason the time the bridegroom will be coming was not clear to everybody. Under those conditions everyone must be ready at any time.

Here's the full parable:

[1] *Then shall the kingdom of heaven be likened unto ten virgins, which took their lamps, and went forth to meet the bridegroom.*

[2] *And five of them were wise, and five were foolish.*

[3] *They that were foolish took their lamps, and took no oil with them:*

⁴ But the wise took oil in their vessels with their lamps.

⁵ While the bridegroom tarried, they all slumbered and slept.

⁶ And at midnight there was a cry made, Behold, the bridegroom cometh; go ye out to meet him.

⁷ Then all those virgins arose, and trimmed their lamps.

⁸ And the foolish said unto the wise, Give us of your oil; for our lamps are gone out.

⁹ But the wise answered, saying, Not so; lest there be not enough for us and you: but go ye rather to them that sell, and buy for yourselves.

¹⁰ And while they went to buy, the bridegroom came; and they that were ready went in with him to the marriage: and the door was shut.

¹¹ Afterward came also the other virgins, saying, Lord, Lord, open to us.

¹² But he answered and said, Verily I say unto you, I know you not.

(Matthew 25:1-12)

Listen to what Jesus said after He had completed the parable:

> ¹³ *Watch therefore, for ye know neither the day nor the hour wherein the Son of man cometh.*

Think of the virgins as saints and believers, like you and me. Is there a mystery formula by which some saints may be left behind? Absolutely not! God is not pulling surprises on anyone. He has made His conditions clear.

Jesus removed the mystery that may be surrounding the reason five were allowed to enter and dine with the groom and five were not allowed. It was about being ready. That is the main theme of this book. It is not to give you some detailed, comprehensive teaching on eschatology. This book is intended to get you ready for what could be your portion in God's plan in the last days of the earth for those who believe in Him

Let's make it simple for all to understand. There are things that get us ready and things that can make one not ready. That is the criteria God is going to use to select who goes up and who is left behind.

Jesus talked about being watchful. Being watchful strongly suggests being alert and living in high expectancy. Imagine that you are at the airport to welcome a relative who travelled and is on his way back home. Fifteen minutes before the flight lands, all your attention is focused on his arrival. If ten planes are landing about the same time, you remain in high alert to see if your relative's flight is the next that lands. You continue with that expectancy in the arrival hall until you see him show up. That is what being watchful is primarily about.

Whatever you are expecting is what captivates your attention until it arrives. Is it possible for someone to know if he will be taken or left behind? Yes, it is possible. God is fair. He has made the conditions clear so no man will be in doubt.

LIKE A THIEF IN THE NIGHT

1. *But of the times and the seasons, brethren, ye have no need that I write unto you.*

2. *For yourselves know perfectly that the day of the Lord so cometh as a thief in the night.*

3. *For when they shall say, Peace and safety; then sudden destruction cometh upon them, as travail upon a woman with child; and they shall not escape.*

4. *But ye, brethren, are not in darkness, that that day should overtake you as a thief.*

5. *Ye are all the children of light, and the children of the day: we are not of the night, nor of darkness.*

6. *Therefore let us not sleep, as do others; but let us watch and be sober.*

> ⁷ For they that sleep sleep in the night; and they that be drunken are drunken in the night.
>
> ⁸ But let us, who are of the day, be sober, putting on the breastplate of faith and love; and for an helmet, the hope of salvation.
>
> ⁹ For God hath not appointed us to wrath, but to obtain salvation by our Lord Jesus Christ,
>
> (1 Thessalonians 5:1-9)

Paul is simply echoing what Jesus said concerning readiness. No man can say the exact date and time of Jesus' coming because Jesus did not tell anyone before He left the earth (Matt 24:36). Just be prepared and be ready for the flight. Have your passport, visa, ticket, and boarding pass; check your things in; be at the airport; be on transit; and anytime the flight comes, you just catch it.

That day will come as a thief in the night. That is the surprise element, and that is the reason why I am alerting you so you are not taken unawares.

BE WISE AND REDEEM THE TIME

> ¹⁴ Wherefore he saith, Awake thou that sleepest, and arise from the dead, and Christ shall give thee light.

> ¹⁵ *See then that ye walk circumspectly, not as fools, but as wise,*
>
> ¹⁶ *Redeeming the time, because the days are evil.*
>
> ¹⁷ *Wherefore be ye not unwise, but understanding what the will of the Lord is.*
>
> ¹⁸ *And be not drunk with wine, wherein is excess; but be filled with the Spirit;*
>
> (Ephesians 5:14-18)

Don't walk as fools, but as wise. This is talking to the church, not unbelievers. He says the days are evil. The Bible said if the time is not shortened, even the very elect will be deceived. The level of deception in the church world in these days is not a joke. People have become like movie stars, and we know movie stars are not real.

Some of the things people are doing to attract crowds and to have a big following are really frightening. The church has become like an industry. People are using all kinds of mechanisms, schemes, devices, and mischiefs to grow their churches. All these are part of the deception Jesus warned. Be careful so you are not caught up in any of them.

What does it mean to be filled with the Spirit? You have to learn to worship every day on your own. Today, we don't worship anymore. We put on music cafes and listen to praise and worship music and videos. We don't know how to worship on our own. There are no spiritual songs in us anymore. We have backslidden.

Someone came to me and said, "I can't pray anymore like I used to pray."

And I said to him, "Don't force it back. In the morning spend about 15 minutes praying. Somewhere in the afternoon, begin again for another 15 minutes. Somewhere in the evening you go at it again. Between the time you go to bed and wake up, when you use the washroom, spend another 10 minutes praying before you go back to bed.

That is how you get yourself filled with the Spirit, worshipping and praying in other tongues. It is not the number of hours you pray at a goal, but the consistency."

I don't pray because I have a need. I pray because prayer is staying in touch; prayer is connecting with God's throne. Prayer is a spiritual vehicle that carries blessings from eternity into time and helps execute the purposes of God.

I have gotten to a place where blessings come to me everywhere. We go to eat in restaurants and when we ask for the bill, we will be told it has been taken care of. When I ask for the one who paid, we never find out. Sometimes these are places where nobody knows me.

Pursue Peace and Holiness

Pursue peace with all people, and holiness, without which no one will see the Lord.

(Hebrews 12:14)

Today, there are no peacemakers anymore. We fight over everything. Years ago, I preached a message and I made reference to a religion that prayed many times a day. It was taken out of context and was misunderstood. When I heard about it I tried to put the records straight. I decided to go find a key leader of that religion to apologize because I didn't mean to demean his religion and faith. I was simply following the Bible principle.

I made him understand that if what I said offended him, then I owed him an apology because none of us is above the Word of God. Later, they came to see me themselves and the leader said he was moved and spoke out of anger, and he apologized. I also stood up and said I was also sorry for what I said, and did not mean to offend them.

Then somebody took only what I said and did not take what he said, and put it on social media to make it look like I went to beg. This went viral and people called asking me to post his apology as well. I did not know why I would do that because

I was not afraid of anyone, and did not have to defend myself. I know sometimes I tend to be too daring, but if I offend somebody, it is required of me to apologize. Whether it is a child or an adult, I am under obligation to apologize.

The greatest freedom I have in life is where I have no reputation to protect. That if people say good things about me, it is good; when they say bad things, it is good; if they don't like me, it is good. Whatever you do to me, it is good. Nothing matters to me anymore. Until you come to a place where the court of public opinion about you does not matter, you are in life imprisonment with hard labor.

> **You must come to the place where the opinions of men, whether good or bad, do not matter anymore. Until you come to that place you are not free. That is the greatest freedom I enjoy; it doesn't matter anymore because I have come to the conclusion that you can never please men.**

It doesn't matter what you do, men will never be satisfied or be pleased. If you have to please someone, please God. As long as you are at peace with God, all else does not matter anymore.

Until you come to a place where you are free of public perception, you are in bondage. I have learned to not please people. I have learned to not be in the good books of anybody. I have learned to accept misrepresentation. It is part of the path I have been called to walk, and I have no defense or explanation. I am what I am by the grace of God.

Christianity is self-denial. You have to deny yourself on a daily basis, and you have to be stripped of self and ego, otherwise you cannot please God. You cannot please man and God at the same time. You cannot serve man and God at the time.

The Bible says we should be at peace with all men. It doesn't matter who they are. If somebody accuses you of offending him or her, just apologize. When I was raising my children, I sometimes spanked them for something I heard they did. If I investigated and later realized I was wrong for spanking them, I just apologized to them and asked for their forgiveness. There are parents who cannot apologize to their children when they are wrong. There are spouses who cannot apologize when they wrong each other. Rendering apology is the path of peace; it is God-ordained and it is a Christian value.

Walk in Purity of Heart

Blessed are the pure in heart: for they shall see God.

(Matthew 5:8)

What is in your heart? For some of us, it might be stubbornness, rebellion, covetousness, disobedience, unforgiveness, hurts, offenses, revenge, arrogance, pride, selfishness, and all kinds of things. Despite all these, we still want God to show Himself to us. You cannot experience God until you are pure at heart.

Get rid of those things in your heart. Get rid of hurt, of offenses; get rid of unforgiveness and bitterness. Get rid of them.

> **If you want to experience God, you have to be pure at heart. It doesn't matter what was done to you, nor how strong your argument may be.**

There is no point in time when bearing grudges against each other will please God. Bearing grudges is actually the path to self-destruction.

David said to the Lord, "Thy word have I hid in mine heart, that I might not sin against thee" (Psa 119:11). He goes on to describe who will be in God's presence:

> ¹ O Lord, who shall sojourn in your tent? Who shall dwell on your holy hill?
>
> ² He who walks blamelessly and does what is right and speaks truth in his heart;
>
> ³ who does not slander with his tongue and does no evil to his neighbor, nor takes up a reproach against his friend;
>
> (Psalm 15:1-3)

There is a place called the holy hill. Not everybody can go there. It takes righteousness to stand there. There are two kinds of righteousness. There is *imputed righteousness*, which you obtained through Christ's atoning work on the cross. This gives you and me right standing before God because of what Jesus did and His blood. We don't have to do anything to obtain it; that is imparted on us.

There is another righteousness called *fulfilled righteousness*. When you pray; when you fast; when you give; when you tithe; when you make vows and honor them; and when you give your first fruit, you walk in fulfilled righteousness. Those are practices that are required of us, and it doesn't matter what confronts you in this life, you are not exempt from walking in fulfilled righteousness.

Liars will not go to heaven. I am not talking about people who lie occasionally. I am talking about perpetual liars; permanent liars, who lie to the point that their lies look like truth.

Hold on to the End

But he who endures to the end shall be saved.

(Matthew 24:13)

One of the reasons I undertook this project is to encourage you to endure to the end. There is a general relaxation about the urgency of the Second Coming. Many do not even have any idea of Second Coming because their pastors have not talked about Jesus' coming in the past several years.

This verse talks about those who endure until the end. What will happen to those who do not? Enduring until the end means you continue holding up your faith in Christ and walking in His ways in the face of anything that happens to you in this life, including rejecting all the offers this world makes to you.

What happens if someone says that he no longer believes in Jesus as his Savior and Lord? What happens if someone gives up faith in Christ and becomes a Muslim, for example? What of those who stop living the Christian life and go back to live in the ways of the world, deeply caught up in the lusts of the flesh, the lusts of the eyes, and the pride of life? Can such people be described as holding on or enduring to the end?

Is there the possibility that someone can lose his salvation?

> **I believe that if you are not conscious of the end times we are in, and what God expects of you in readiness for the Second Coming, there is the possibility that even though you are saved you will fall by the wayside and lose your salvation.**

He that is saved and holds on and endures to the end, the same shall keep his salvation. Being caught up in the air when Jesus comes is not automatic. That is why God's Word instructs us to work out our own salvation with fear and trembling.

I am working at it; every now and then I confess that, "Jesus Christ is Lord." The Bible says that, "For whosoever shall call upon the name of the Lord shall be saved" (Rom 10:13).

I, therefore, confess Jesus as my Lord and Savior. I confess what I believe in my heart, that God has raised Him from the dead. I confess my salvation every now and then just to assure my subconscious.

8.
WHAT IF YOU MISS THE RAPTURE?

It is fearsome if you take your time to study what happens to those who don't make the rapture, those who don't make that flight. There is only one flight from time into eternity, and those who miss that one flight can only make it by becoming martyrs of Christ. They will have to be beheaded to make that journey.

THE GREAT TRIBULATION

My assignment is to help you avoid going through the great tribulation. There certainly is a period the Bible calls "the tribulation". This is what Jesus said:

> *For then there will be great tribulation, such as has not been since the beginning of the world until this time, no, nor ever shall be.*
>
> *(Matthew 24:21)*

Several years before Jesus walked on this earth, Daniel gave a grand summary of what those who miss the flight will go through:

> *And at that time shall Michael stand up, the great prince which standeth for the children of thy people: and there shall be a time of trouble, such as never was since there was a nation even to that same time: and at that time thy people shall be delivered, every one that shall be found written in the book.*
>
> *(Daniel 12:1)*

The *"children of your people"* refers to the people of Israel. Your name must be in the book. Anyone whose name is in the book shall be delivered.

Here's another presentation by the Apostle John:

> [16] *Also it causes all, both small and great, both rich and poor, both free and slave, to be marked on the right hand or the forehead,*
>
> [17] *so that no one can buy or sell unless he has the mark, that is, the name of the beast or the number of its name.*
>
> [18] *This calls for wisdom: let the one who has understanding calculate the number of the beast, for it is the number of a man, and his number is 666.*
>
> *(Revelation 13:16-18)*

These passages describe what will happen to those who miss the rapture. You can't buy or sell; you can't confess the name of Jesus at that time and you can't repent. Anyone who lives after the rapture must have the mark of the beast to be able to buy or sell.

Anyone who takes the mark of the beast renounces Jesus and becomes a property of the beast, the devil. They will not make it to heaven, according to Scripture, and the Scriptures cannot be broken.

I am not going to argue the Scriptures. I know God is the God of love. People say He is a good God and a God of love, and He understands. No, God does not understand why you would take the mark of the beast when you have the opportunity today to give your life to Christ. Those who refuse to take the mark of the beast will only make it by becoming martyrs for Jesus. They will be beheaded. It is going to happen.

SEVEN PLAGUES

Read the following account in the Book of Revelation that describes some of the things that will happen during the tribulation:

> 1 Then I heard a loud voice from the temple telling the seven angels, "Go and pour out on

the earth the seven bowls of the wrath of God."

2. So the first angel went and poured out his bowl on the earth, and harmful and painful sores came upon the people who bore the mark of the beast and worshiped its image.

3. The second angel poured out his bowl into the sea, and it became like the blood of a corpse, and every living thing died that was in the sea.

4. The third angel poured out his bowl into the rivers and the springs of water, and they became blood.

5. And I heard the angel in charge of the waters say, "Just are you, O Holy One, who is and who was, for you brought these judgments.

6. For they have shed the blood of saints and prophets, and you have given them blood to drink. It is what they deserve!"

7. And I heard the altar saying, "Yes, Lord God the Almighty, true and just are your judgments!"

8. The fourth angel poured out his bowl on the sun, and it was allowed to scorch people with fire.

9. They were scorched by the fierce heat, and they cursed the name of God who had

power over these plagues. They did not repent and give him glory.

¹⁰ *The fifth angel poured out his bowl on the throne of the beast, and its kingdom was plunged into darkness. People gnawed their tongues in anguish*

¹¹ *and cursed the God of heaven for their pain and sores. They did not repent of their deeds.*

¹² *The sixth angel poured out his bowl on the great river Euphrates, and its water was dried up, to prepare the way for the kings from the east*

¹³ *And I saw, coming out of the mouth of the dragon and out of the mouth of the beast and out of the mouth of the false prophet, three unclean spirits like frogs.*

¹⁴ *For they are demonic spirits, performing signs, who go abroad to the kings of the whole world, to assemble them for battle on the great day of God the Almighty.*

¹⁵ *("Behold, I am coming like a thief! Blessed is the one who stays awake, keeping his garments on, that he may not go about naked and be seen exposed!")*

¹⁶ *And they assembled them at the place that in Hebrew is called Armageddon.*

> ¹⁷ *The seventh angel poured out his bowl into the air, and a loud voice came out of the temple, from the throne, saying, "It is done!"*
>
> ¹⁸ *And there were flashes of lightning, rumblings,[c] peals of thunder, and a great earthquake such as there had never been since man was on the earth, so great was that earthquake.*
>
> ¹⁹ *The great city was split into three parts, and the cities of the nations fell, and God remembered Babylon the great, to make her drain the cup of the wine of the fury of his wrath*
>
> ²⁰ *And every island fled away, and no mountains were to be found*
>
> ²¹ *And great hailstones, about one hundred pounds each, fell from heaven on people; and they cursed God for the plague of the hail, because the plague was so severe.*
>
> (Revelation 16:1-21)

This passage speaks for itself. It talks of seven plagues that will come upon the earth as soon as the church and the Holy Ghost leave the earth. It is part of the 14 prophecies yet to be fulfilled. It clearly outlines what will happen to those who don't make the rapture.

All of us who have believed are not part of those who will be faced with taking the mark of the beast. There is a punishment and a judgment that will hit those who take the mark of the beast because it is a compromise. They loved their lives, and because of that, they renounced Jesus and compromised their faith and conviction, and accepted the mark of the beast that they might live.

The people did not repent because the dispensation of grace had ended. The Holy Spirit had left, so there was no way to repent even if they wanted to. It was too late. That is very scary. It scares me to read some of these Scriptures. I don't know what is in your heart, but it scares me. The reason repentance is critical is because it gives God glory.

When we turn around and go to Him and say, "God, I have missed it. I never intended to offend or hurt You. I never intended to take You for granted. Help me. I'll do right. I'll do well."

God will take you in His arms. You don't need tribulation.

Anytime you see the beast that is Satan, the devil. There will be great pain and torture to the point where they curse God because they can't repent and the pain won't stop. The sores won't go away, and repentance is over. So all they will do is curse God.

The water of the river Euphrates has to be dried up to make way for Russia and the kings of the east to come together against Israel in the battle of Armageddon, before Revelation 19, when we come back. You have to be among those who are coming back in Revelation 19. You must ride on those white horses. You can't miss that one. That is the real show. I look forward to it. I don't know about you.

To learn more about what happens to those who miss the rapture, take time to read the passage below in Revelation 17:

> 1 Then one of the seven angels who had the seven bowls came and said to me, "Come, I will show you the judgment of the great prostitute who is seated on many waters,
>
> 2 with whom the kings of the earth have committed sexual immorality, and with the wine of whose sexual immorality the dwellers on earth have become drunk."
>
> 3 And he carried me away in the Spirit into a wilderness, and I saw a woman sitting on a scarlet beast that was full of blasphemous names, and it had seven heads and ten horns.
>
> 4 The woman was arrayed in purple and scarlet, and adorned with gold and jewels and pearls, holding in her hand a golden cup full of

abominations and the impurities of her sexual immorality.

⁵ And on her forehead was written a name of mystery: "Babylon the great, mother of prostitutes and of earth's abominations.

⁶ And I saw the woman, drunk with the blood of the saints, the blood of the martyrs of Jesus. When I saw her, I marveled greatly.

⁷ But the angel said to me, "Why do you marvel? I will tell you the mystery of the woman, and of the beast with seven heads and ten horns that carries her.

⁸ The beast that you saw was, and is not, and is about to rise from the bottomless pit and go to destruction. And the dwellers on earth whose names have not been written in the book of life from the foundation of the world will marvel to see the beast, because it was and is not and is to come.

⁹ This calls for a mind with wisdom: the seven heads are seven mountains on which the woman is seated;

¹⁰ they are also seven kings, five of whom have fallen, one is, the other has not yet come, and when he does come he must remain only a little while.

¹¹ As for the beast that was and is not, it is an eighth but it belongs to the seven, and it goes to destruction.

¹² And the ten horns that you saw are ten kings who have not yet received royal power, but they are to receive authority as kings for one hour, together with the beast.

¹³ These are of one mind, and they hand over their power and authority to the beast.

¹⁴ They will make war on the Lamb, and the Lamb will conquer them, for he is Lord of lords and King of kings, and those with him are called and chosen and faithful."

¹⁵ And the angel said to me, "The waters that you saw, where the prostitute is seated, are peoples and multitudes and nations and languages.

¹⁶ And the ten horns that you saw, they and the beast will hate the prostitute. They will make her desolate and naked, and devour her flesh and burn her up with fire,

¹⁷ for God has put it into their hearts to carry out his purpose by being of one mind and handing over their royal power to the beast, until the words of God are fulfilled.

¹⁸ And the woman that you saw is the great city that has dominion over the kings of the earth."

There are believers who don't even know what the Scripture is saying. That is why I wanted us to read all the passages so you see that it is not my word, but the Word of the Lord.

Those who don't make it and take the mark of the beast will be killed but they will be resurrected during the thousand years when we come before the second resurrection.

> **The fearful thing is that Christianity is the only religion or kingdom where the citizens of faith don't care about their kingdom and their religion. They are very selfish; they care about themselves.**

You and I won't be there during this tribulation. Let me establish something because there are two schools of thought. One school of thought claims that the church will see the tribulation and live in the midst of it. The second school of thought believes that the church will be taken before the great tribulation.

I don't care if we will see the great tribulation and be taken within it, or if we will be taken before. What I care about is for us to be ready and have our names confirmed on heaven's manifest. I care that, whether it is before or in the midst of it, we don't miss the flight.

What I know is that it is a terrible thing for anyone to miss the flight to H-E-A-V-E-N.

9.
JUDGMENT AFTER DEATH

> [30] The times of ignorance God overlooked, but now he commands all people everywhere to repent,
>
> [31] because he has fixed a day on which he will judge the world in righteousness by a man whom he has appointed; and of this he has given assurance to all by raising him from the dead."
>
> (Acts 17:30-31)
>
> [27] And just as it is appointed for man to die once, and after that comes judgment,
>
> [28] so Christ, having been offered once to bear the sins of many, will appear a second time, not to deal with sin but to save those who are eagerly waiting for him.
>
> (Hebrews 9:27-28)

We must all understand that we are on this earth not by chance. Each of us was created and endowed by God for a purpose. Our individual purposes look alike in many ways, yet are unique to each of us. Jesus spoke of a parable where a king gave talents to his servants prior to embarking on a journey. If you know the story, you realize that He did not expect the same quantum of profits from His servants; rather He demanded results in proportion to the number of talents he gave each of them.

The truth no man can run away from is that each of us will give account of ourselves to God (Rom 14:12). The Bible calls this judgment. We all shall be judged. In this chapter, I want to discuss the judgment of God to enable us to prepare for it because it is on the way.

The passages above establish the reality of judgment that all men will face God one day to give account of how we lived.

The Bible, however, makes distinctions between the judgments that are coming on humanity.

First, there is the judgment of those who rejected Jesus Christ outright, and refused to acknowledge him as Lord and Savior. They will face judgment leading unto condemnation. Their end will be in the lake of fire together with Satan and his angels. This will take place at the judgment throne of God.

The second judgment will be for those who accepted Jesus Christ as Savior; those that will be raptured when Jesus return to the earth again. It will take place at the judgment seat of Christ.

It is interesting that the two passages above all link the eternal judgment to Jesus and His resurrection. They establish that God has committed judgment to His Son who walked our earth in our human form.

How can anyone compare Jesus with anyone else dead or alive? All men will stand before Him in judgment one day. He certainly must be in His own class. No wonder we worship Him and honor Him above all things.

JUDGMENT THRONE OF GOD

> 11 Then I saw a great white throne and him who was seated on it. From his presence earth and sky fled away, and no place was found for them.
>
> 12 And I saw the dead, great and small, standing before the throne, and books were opened. Then another book was opened, which is the book of life. And the dead were judged by what was written in the books, according to what they had done.
>
> 13 And the sea gave up the dead who were in it, Death and Hades gave up the dead who were in them, and they were judged, each one of them, according to what they had done.

> ¹⁴ Then Death and Hades were thrown into the lake of fire. This is the second death, the lake of fire.
>
> ¹⁵ And if anyone's name was not found written in the book of life, he was thrown into the lake of fire.
>
> (Revelation 20:11-15)

This passage talks about both the small and great standing before God. This is a different judgment. This does not apply to you and I who hold our faith in Jesus unto the end. Ours is different.

Remember that death itself will be judged and hell will be judged. The final destiny for Satan and his angels and all those who refused Christ and didn't live according to the rules is not the grave (which is also hades); it is the lake of fire. So death and hades are transitional and the two of them will be judged and cast into the lake of fire that was prepared for Satan and his angels. Please remember that the lake of fire or hell was never intended to be for any man. That was never God's intention. It was not made for man, but Satan and his angels.

> The devil who deceived them, was cast into the lake of fire and brimstone where the beast and the false prophet are. And they will be tormented day and night forever and ever.

(Revelation 20:10)

Sometimes people call me and say we have to do something about the false prophets, and I reply that it's not my place to do anything about them. Their destinies have already been determined. They can still repent but I am not speaking against them nor touching them. Those who follow them will share also in their judgment. The Word of God is very clear about it.

> ¹⁵ Then the kings of the earth and the great ones and the generals and the rich and the powerful, and everyone, slave and free, hid themselves in the caves and among the rocks of the mountains,
>
> ¹⁶ calling to the mountains and rocks, "Fall on us and hide us from the face of him who is seated on the throne, and from the wrath of the Lamb,
>
> ¹⁷ for the great day of their wrath has come, and who can stand?"

(Revelation 6:15-17)

Nothing will stand on that day, and what baffles me is the fact that the Bible did not say the dragon and the lion, but talks about the wrath of the Lamb. This is the same Lamb whom the Bible said takes away the sin of this world. Now, at this particular time the Lamb put on the robe and the judgment of vengeance and wrath. The Lamb, not the lion, becomes angry because too much has been taken for granted for far too long.

The Bible asks the question, "Who shall stand"? There is no captain, no general, no small, no great, no wealthy, and no intellectual; no matter who you are. Connection won't stand, background won't stand; the color of your skin won't stand; the school you attended won't stand; the family you are connected to won't stand. It doesn't matter whom you know, who you are, or where you come from. Nobody will be able to stand the anger of the Lamb on that day.

The Bible says they cried for the mountains and the hills to fall on them and to hide them from the wrath of the Lamb. I don't want to face the anger and wrath of the Lamb. I don't know about you, it is your decision.

JUDGMENT SEAT OF CHRIST

This is the second type of judgment.

> 6 So we are always of good courage. We know that while we are at home in the body we are away from the Lord,
>
> 7 for we walk by faith, not by sight.

> ⁸ *Yes, we are of good courage, and we would rather be away from the body and at home with the Lord.*
>
> ⁹ *So whether we are at home or away, we make it our aim to please him.*
>
> ¹⁰ *For we must all appear before the judgment seat of Christ, so that each one may receive what is due for what he has done in the body, whether good or evil.*
>
> *(2 Corinthians 5:6-10)*

We must all; not some; not few; for we must all appear before Him. This is referring to believers and those who make the rapture, and those that remain after the rapture, who don't take the mark of the beast, also the martyrs of Christ. This has to be for believers.

This is not a judgment unto condemnation. It is a time of accountability. It is about judgment to account for what we did with our time, with our body, and with the money that came into our hands.

Whatever resources we are given are for the purposes of the gospel, for the saving of souls to expand the course of His church. Jesus said "… and upon this rock I will build my church; and the gates of hell shall not prevail against it" (Matt 16:18).

Jesus is not building your business. He is not building my business. He is building His church. God's number one priority and interest in this world and in this nation is His church and His people, and nothing else comes close to that.

> **Knowing that a day of reckoning is coming for all of us, we must not take life for granted.**

On that day we all, members of the choir, whatever role you play, businessman, business woman, politician, and so on, we will all stand before the judgment seat of Christ as believers. It's a day of accountability and we shall answer, and on that day we cannot fool God; we cannot lie. Please stop thinking that your life is your own. You don't have any life. You don't own anything. You could lose the life you think is yours today.

On the day of judgment, you will hear things that will amaze you because we will all come before the judgment seat of Christ, and everybody will give an account of what we did with our body, and what we did with our time, and what we did with the resources that were given to us; whether we used them for the kingdom, for the church, or for ourselves. On that day, mysteries and secrets will be revealed.

Our works shall be tested by fire. Some will stand the test some will not. The Apostle Paul, therefore, warns us how we build and with what materials we build. Here's what he said:

> [12] Now if anyone builds on the foundation with gold, silver, precious stones, wood, hay, straw—
>
> [13] each one's work will become manifest, for the Day will disclose it, because it will be revealed by fire, and the fire will test what sort of work each one has done.
>
> [14] If the work that anyone has built on the foundation survives, he will receive a reward.
>
> [15] If anyone's work is burned up, he will suffer loss, though he himself will be saved, but only as through fire.
>
> (1 Corinthians 3:12-15)

We have no idea what it means for your work to suffer loss on that day. Certainly it will not be fun. That is even more the reason we should be mindful how we build, and with what we build. There is enough Scripture that shows what to do to ensure that our works will survive the heat with which they will be tried. Simply follow the Scripture and you will be fine.

Epilogue:
My Foretaste of Heaven

This generation has come to a place that we apologize for serving God. I have no apology for serving God. I am what I am by the grace of God. I was nothing and nobody; raised in the ghettos of Accra; grew up in Wa; and lived in downtown Bolgatanga. And somebody had mercy on me and moved me from nowhere to somewhere; made something out of nothing; made a somebody out of a nobody.

People ask me all the time, the reason for my success. They want to know the secret. I say that I have no secret and I am not yet successful because success is not where you are today. Success has nothing to do with money or material gains. Success has nothing to do with accolades. It has nothing to do with relevance or receiving awards, where they talk about all your achievements and not your mistakes in life.

I tell my children the reason I advise them and they must listen to me is because I have made more mistakes in life than I have done the right things, and I have failed many more times than I won. That's why I don't like receiving awards. At the place of award they talk about all your achievements, but that is not the truth about my life because I have had many failures, many betrayals, many setbacks, and many disappointments. I've dealt with so much more shame and misrepresentation than achievements. So, if you want to award me be willing and be ready to talk about some of my scandals, some of my stigma, some of my disappointments, and some of my reproaches. Then, the award would be complete. But, if you are only talking about my achievement, you don't know me!

Success has nothing to do with how many churches you have; how many services you run; or who comes or does not come to your church. It has nothing to do with how many people you have on your Facebook, or how big you are on social media. It has nothing to do with how deep your pocket is or might be. It has nothing to do with the fact that you are a financial mogul, or you are an oil sheikh or a business magnate or business tycoon. It has nothing to do with where you are today or your investments in life or the assets you have. True success has to do with how you end the race.

I've seen millionaires who, after a while, didn't even have money to buy food. I was talking to one of them, a young man. By the age of 21 he was a multi-millionaire. His wife came to see me recently because they did not have money for food and the young man had asked her to come see me for help. So money is not everything, but relationships can take you places where money cannot. Therefore, whenever you get money, do not despise relationships because you never know whom you'll need tomorrow. True success is how you finish, and I intend to finish well. I'm determined to finish well. I have not yet attained, like Paul said in Philippians 3:13:

> **Brethren, I count not myself to have apprehended: but this one thing I do, forgetting those things which are behind, and reaching forth unto those things which are before**

Paul said that he didn't count himself as one who has yet attained, or arrived, or perfected, or made it. I'm still being made. Preaching for over 40 years and I'm still on the roads; I haven't yet attained. It is a daily crucifixion and a daily sanctification and daily purity and daily self-examination of your heart and your motives. It's a daily thing. I know some of you have arrived, but I haven't. I'm still working on myself.

When I was taken to heaven I had so many surprises, things I can't even talk about because I can't make sense out of it. And as much as I saw it, I still don't fully understand it. I believe that there are a lot of messages in it for me personally and God is telling me some things, and I am processing them.

I saw cars in heaven, and I saw an elder in heaven, and he was riding a beautiful car, and it was shining, and I was shocked to see cars in heaven.

Then the angel said to me, "Have you not read and been told that the streets of heaven are made up of gold?"

Then it made sense that streets are made for cars.

I was in another part of heaven and I saw a lot of people, great people when they were on earth. I was told that these were mighty people who did mighty deeds for God when they were on earth but their motives were wrong. They did it out of covetousness; they did it to spite others; they did it for self-relevance, and not for the glory of God. So even though they made it to heaven, their works were burned by the fire and most of them were living in dormitories like students.

Then I was taken to another place and was shown a beautiful city and the angel said, "This is the city of T. L. Osborn."

I said, "That is my grandfather in the faith."

It was a city. T.L. Osborn was not on any popular television station, nobody knew him. He was preaching in Africa and India, in places that you and I would not go. He was preaching and winning souls for the kingdom.

I was travelling one time and the spirit asked me to reroute my flight. So I called and asked them to do that because perhaps God wanted to show me something. In Chicago, my flight delayed for two hours. So I started talking to God, but He did not say anything. You see, God does not owe us any explanation. God commands, He does not suggest.

I decided to get something and while I was in the line, the Spirit told me to lift up my eyes, and when I did, I saw T. L. Osborn, and the Spirit told me to go talk to him. So I went over and we started talking. I told him about his city that I saw in heaven and he smiled, and said, "That is why, over 80 years, I am still preaching and winning souls."

Heaven is not some small town. Heaven is loaded and I am not living for here only; I am living for here after. The amazing thing is that when people get blessed or promoted and you try to get in touch with them, they won't even return your calls because they think you need something from them. But I return peoples' calls when I miss their calls. Sometimes I don't feel like it, but O man, who are you?

We must come to a place in our lives where we treat human beings, no matter who they are, as human beings. When we come to a place where we despise and look down on people because of where or who we are, we must know that time changes and it's a matter of time. Treat human beings as human beings because you never know what tomorrow will bring.

A time will come when conducting business as usual, and they will say, "Peace, everything is fine. Don't mind this preacher. Nothing is going to happen."

That is none of my responsibility. I will continue to preach.

www.ingramcontent.com/pod-product-compliance
Lightning Source LLC
Chambersburg PA
CBHW050645160426
43194CB00010B/1821